HISTORY FOR MEN

INTERESTING SHORT STORIES FACTS AND TRIVIA

NO WAY THAT HAPPENED

BN WILLIAM

BNW PUBLISH

This book is a work of nonfiction. Every effort has been made to ensure accuracy at the time of publication. Some dialogue and details have been lightly adapted for clarity.

For permissions or inquiries, contact: **BNW Publishing**

Contents, Because History Refuses to Be Linear

Before you dive in, here's a little gift: scan the QR code and join our FREE weekly newsletter.

Every week you'll get fresh quizzes, mind-bending facts, and hilarious history stories delivered straight to your inbox. It's like keeping the fun of this book going, long after you've closed the cover.

We'll even send you an exclusive peek at our Amazon #1 Bestseller, Shut the Fact Up.

No spam, no boring stuff. Just facts that surprise, delight, and occasionally make you laugh out loud.

Scan the QR code and start your weekly trivia fix today!

History, Some Assembly (and Pop Quizzes) Required

Welcome to the madhouse of history. These aren't the tidy timelines your teachers forced on you; this is the messy, funny, sometimes downright bizarre side of the past. You'll get short, snappy stories that prove truth really is stranger than fiction.

And once you've filled your head with these wild tales, it's time to test it. At the back of the book, you'll find Pop Quizzes, not the boring kind, but quick-fire brain benders that ask you to put events in order, match the right characters, and spot who said what. Think of them as history's equivalent of a pub quiz, only with less beer spilled on the table.

So read on, laugh a little, raise your eyebrows a lot, and when you think you've got it all down... flip to the quizzes and test your history.

From Alchemy to Atrocity, The Tale of Chlorine Gas

"Bent double, like old beggars under sacks,
Knock-kneed, coughing like hags, we cursed through sludge,
Till on the haunting flares we turned our backs
And towards our distant rest began to trudge.
Men marched asleep. Many had lost their boots
But limped on, blood-shod. All went lame; all blind;
Drunk with fatigue; deaf even to the hoots
Of tired, outstripped Five-Nines that dropped behind.

Gas! Gas! Quick, boys! An ecstasy of fumbling,
Fitting the clumsy helmets just in time;
But someone still was yelling out and stumbling,
And flound'ring like a man in fire or lime...
Dim, through the misty panes and thick green light,
As under a green sea, I saw him drowning."

Wilfred Owen wrote those lines after witnessing gas attacks on the Western Front. His poem "Dulce et Decorum Est" ends with bitter words about "the old lie" that it is sweet and honorable to die for one's country. Owen knew better. He'd watched men drown in poison gas while fighting for "some corner of a foreign field that is forever England." There was nothing sweet about choking to death on your own liquefied lungs, nothing honorable about drowning in a green sea of chemical death far from home.

The story of that green sea begins not in the trenches of Belgium, but in a Swedish laboratory 141 years earlier, where a curious chemist had no idea he was creating the future of warfare.

The Chemist Who Chose War

On a spring afternoon in 1774, Carl Wilhelm Scheele mixed manganese dioxide with muriatic acid and watched something extraordinary happen. A greenish-yellow gas hissed from his apparatus, sharp and acrid, with the strangest property: it bleached everything it touched. Scheele called his discovery "dephlogisticated muriatic acid air," a name that sounds like something a wizard might mumble while stirring a cauldron. He had no idea he'd just unleashed one of chemistry's most Jekyll-and-Hyde substances.

What Scheele had discovered was chlorine, though it would take another 36 years before Humphry Davy gave it that name in 1810, derived from the Greek word "chloros" meaning pale green or yellow-green. For decades, chlorine remained a laboratory curiosity, a party trick for chemists who enjoyed watching it turn colored paper white. It seemed harmless enough, even beneficial. By the mid-1800s, chlorine was cleaning drinking water and bleaching textiles, quietly saving thousands of lives through disinfection. It was chemistry's helpful little helper, scrubbing away disease and grime with equal efficiency.

Then came Fritz Haber. His work on synthesizing ammonia for fertilizer had helped feed millions, earning him Nobel Prize recognition. But when World War I trapped Germany in the bloody stalemate of trench warfare, Haber had a radical idea. Turn chemistry into a weapon.

Haber wasn't some mad scientist cackling over test tubes. He was a patriot who genuinely believed that deploying poison gas would shorten the war and ultimately save lives. "Death is death, whether it comes from a bullet or from gas," he argued. To him, chlorine gas was simply a more efficient bullet, a technological advancement that would break the deadlock consuming an entire generation.

His wife, Clara Immerwahr, also a chemist, saw things differently. She understood the science as well as her husband did, but grasped something he seemed to miss. The moral line between healing and harming. Clara had spent her career fighting for women's rights in science, breaking barriers in a male-dominated field. Now she watched her husband use their shared knowledge to break something far more fundamental.

The couple's arguments grew heated as Haber threw himself into weaponizing chlorine. He calculated lethal concentrations with the same methodical precision he'd once applied to fertilizer chemistry. Clara pleaded with him to stop, arguing that science should serve humanity, not slaughter it. But Haber was convinced he was serving humanity by ending the war faster.

Their debate would echo through the decades. Where should the line be drawn when science meets warfare? It's a question that would resurface in treaty negotiations, in Obama and Cameron's red line over Syrian chemical attacks, and in every laboratory where researchers must choose between discovery and destruction.

The Green Cloud of Ypres

April 22, 1915, dawned clear and still near the Belgian town of Ypres. German troops had spent weeks positioning over 5,000 steel cylinders along their front lines, waiting for the wind to shift in their favor. Each cylinder contained chlorine gas under pressure, 168 tons in total, enough to create a lethal cloud several miles wide.

At 5:00 PM, when the wind finally turned toward Allied lines, German soldiers opened the valves. What happened next had never been seen in human warfare. A yellow-green wall of gas, denser than air, rolled across no man's land like a slow-motion tsunami of death. Birds fell from the sky as the cloud passed beneath them. The smell hit first, a mixture of pepper and pineapple that masked something far more sinister.

The French colonial troops in the gas's path had no idea what they were seeing. Military doctrine had prepared them for bullets, shells, and bayonets, not clouds of chemical death. They had no masks, no training, no defense except instinct. Some tried to flee, others held wet cloths over their faces, a few attempted to burrow into the earth itself.

It didn't matter. Chlorine gas is heavier than air, so it poured into trenches like liquid poison, seeking out every hiding place. The first breath brought panic. The sweet, cloying smell of pineapple mixed with pepper burned the nostrils, followed immediately by a sensation like swallowing fire. Within seconds, the throat began to constrict and burn. Then came the desperate gasping as the gas reacted with moisture in their lungs to form hydrochloric acid.

"Gas! Gas! Quick, boys!" The frantic cry from Owen's poem became reality, but there were no clumsy helmets to fumble for, no salvation. Their own breath became their enemy, turning their airways into chemical burns from the inside out. Men clawed at their throats, eyes streaming, lungs filling with fluid as they drowned in their own bodies' desperate attempts to fight the poison. The drowning wasn't metaphorical - it was literal suffocation as blood-tinged foam bubbled from their mouths.

The immediate death toll was staggering: over 800 soldiers killed in the first few minutes, with thousands more injured. Many of those who survived the initial attack suffered permanent lung damage, spending the rest of their shortened lives struggling for breath. The gas had done exactly what Haber intended, punching a gaping hole in Allied lines that German troops quickly exploited.

But the attack's success came with an unexpected problem. Even the Germans were shocked by what they'd unleashed. Many German soldiers, witnessing the agonizing deaths they'd caused, found themselves psychologically scarred by their own weapon. The chlorine had killed efficiently, but it had also killed something else: the last pretense that war could be civilized.

The Price of Innovation

Clara Immerwahr attended a dinner party celebrating her husband's successful gas attack. As guests toasted Haber's scientific achievement and its potential to end the war, Clara quietly slipped away. She went to their garden, took her husband's service revolver, and shot herself in the heart. She died in the arms of their 13-year-old son, who had run outside when he heard the gunshot.

The next day, Haber left for the Eastern Front to oversee more gas attacks. He either couldn't or wouldn't see the connection between his wife's suicide and his work. To him, Clara had simply succumbed to the strain of wartime, another casualty of the conflict he was trying to end. He never acknowledged that she might have been the first victim of chemical warfare, destroyed not by gas but by the moral horror of what science could become.

Clara's death barely slowed the chemical arms race she had died protesting. The Allies quickly developed their own poison gas weapons, improving on Haber's chlorine with deadlier agents like phosgene and mustard gas. What had started as Germany's secret weapon became the signature horror of World War I, responsible for over 1.3 million casualties by war's end.

Haber had deployed chlorine to end the war quickly and humanely. Instead, he'd introduced a new form of suffering that prolonged the conflict. The gas attacks didn't break the stalemate, they just added a new dimension of terror to it.

Adding to the moral complexity, Haber was awarded the 1918 Nobel Prize in Chemistry for the Haber-Bosch process that synthesized ammonia for fertilizer production. Many Allied scientists boycotted the ceremony and condemned the Swedish Academy for recognizing the man responsible for the first use of chemical weapons. Here was Haber being honored for a process that helped feed millions while simultaneously being reviled for weaponizing chemistry.

The tragedy extended into the next generation. Hermann Haber, who had witnessed his mother's suicide at age 13, would later adopt his mother's maiden name, perhaps to distance himself from his father's infamous reputation. Deeply affected by both his mother's death and his father's work, Hermann would also take his own life years later. There's an old saying that "the sins of the fathers are visited upon the children," and Hermann's tragedy seemed to prove that some wounds pass through generations like a genetic inheritance. Fritz Haber's choices had rippled far beyond the battlefields of Ypres, destroying his family line as surely as his chlorine gas had destroyed enemy trenches.

Chemistry's Moral Reckoning

World War I ended not because of chemical weapons but despite them. The gas attacks had failed to deliver the quick victory Haber promised, serving instead as a gruesome sideshow to four years of unprecedented carnage. The Allies had quickly adapted, developing their own gas weapons and better protective equipment. What had started as Germany's technological advantage became a mutual horror that changed nothing strategically. Military leaders on both sides realized that gas attacks were more trouble than they were worth, requiring perfect weather conditions and often backfiring when the wind shifted.

The revulsion was so universal that the international community moved quickly to ban chemical weapons entirely. The Geneva Protocol of 1925, officially titled the "Protocol for the Prohibition of the Use in War of Asphyxiating, Poisonous or Other Gases, and of Bacteriological Methods of Warfare," was signed by 44 nations initially and eventually ratified by most countries worldwide. The treaty prohibited the use of chemical and biological weapons in warfare but notably did not ban their production or stockpiling, a loophole that would prove problematic in later decades. Many signatories also reserved the right to retaliate with chemical weapons if attacked first, effectively making it a "no first use" agreement rather than a complete ban. The Geneva Protocol of 1925 prohibited the use of poison gas in warfare, one of the first successful attempts to place moral limits on military technology. It was a direct response to the horrors of Ypres and the dozens of gas attacks that followed.

When the Nazis rose to power, they had no use for a Jewish scientist, regardless of his service to the Fatherland. Haber died in exile in Switzerland in 1934, his health broken and his legacy forever tainted by the green clouds of Ypres.

Lines in the Sand, Written in Gas

The Geneva Protocol of 1925 established a moral boundary that would be tested repeatedly over the following century. Italy used mustard gas against Ethiopian forces in 1935-36, delivering it through aerial bombs and spray tanks to terrorize both soldiers and civilians. Despite Emperor Haile Selassie's direct appeals to the League of Nations, the international community imposed only limited economic sanctions and failed to act decisively. The message was clear: moral boundaries meant little when powerful nations chose to ignore them.

Japan's chemical warfare program was even more systematic and secret. Unit 731 conducted brutal human experiments with mustard gas, cyanides, and nerve agents on prisoners, then deployed these weapons extensively across China. The program was so clandestine that its full scope wasn't revealed until decades after the war, contributing to hundreds of thousands of casualties in what amounted to large-scale field trials of chemical terror.

The most significant test came during the Iran-Iraq War (1980-1988), when Saddam Hussein's forces used chemical weapons against Iranian troops and Iraqi Kurdish civilians. The Halabja massacre in 1988 killed an estimated 5,000 Kurdish civilians in a single day with a cocktail of mustard gas, sarin, and tabun. The international response was muted, revealing how easily moral lines could be crossed when geopolitical interests were at stake.

Then came Syria. When Bashar al-Assad's regime used chlorine gas and sarin against Syrian civilians in 2013, it triggered the crisis Clara and Fritz had debated a century earlier. Obama and Cameron declared chemical weapons use a "red line" that would trigger military intervention. But when the moment came, political calculations overrode moral imperatives. Western publics, exhausted by the disastrous interventions in Iraq and Afghanistan, had no appetite for another Middle Eastern war. The red line wavered, then dissolved entirely. History doesn't repeat, but it rhymes: just as the League of Nations had failed to act decisively against Italy's chemical attacks in Ethiopia, the international community once again chose political expedience over moral enforcement.

Assad's forces perfected what became known as "poor man's chemical weapons," dropping crude barrel bombs filled with chlorine cylinders from helicopters. When these bombs detonate, they release toxic gas in a simple but effective terror tactic. Unlike sophisticated nerve agents, chlorine is everywhere, readily available for "legitimate" industrial purposes. The same element that Scheele discovered in 1774, that saves millions through water purification, had once again become a weapon of terror.

Clara Immerwahr's desperate attempt to draw a moral line in 1915 echoes through these modern failures. She understood what many still struggle to accept: scientific knowledge carries moral weight, and those who wield it cannot hide behind claims of neutrality. Whether in a German laboratory in 1915, the League of Nations' chambers in 1936, or the White House situation room in 2013, the choice remains the same. Science can heal or it can harm, but it can never be innocent. And those who hold power to enforce moral boundaries face the same test Clara understood: some lines are worth defending, whatever the political cost.

Wilfred Owen wrote of men drowning "under a green sea" of chlorine gas, and that green sea still claims victims today. Chemical weapons may kill fewer people than nuclear bombs or conventional warfare, but the manner of death remains uniquely horrific. The soldiers at Ypres and the children in Syrian hospitals shared the same agonizing end: drowning in their own liquefied lungs, gasping for air that had turned to poison. Some weapons kill efficiently. Chemical weapons kill cruelly. That distinction matters, even if the dead can't tell the difference.

Did You Know?

The first gas masks weren't masks at all, Canadian troops at Ypres urinated on handkerchiefs and held them over their faces. The ammonia in urine neutralized chlorine gas just enough to survive. Sometimes salvation comes from the strangest sources.

Chlorine bleach in your laundry room is essentially domesticated chemical warfare, the same compound that killed thousands now whitens your socks at a concentration of 3-6% instead of the lethal doses used in WWI.

Fritz Haber's institute later employed scientists who fled Nazi Germany, including several who worked on the Manhattan Project. The same building that weaponized chemistry helped create the scientists who would defeat Haber's homeland.

The Great Stink of 1184, A Royal Flush Gone Wrong

On July 26, 1184, the cream of German nobility gathered in Erfurt for what they assumed would be another tedious political assembly. This was medieval Germany at its peak, a patchwork of duchies, bishoprics, and free cities that somehow functioned as the Holy Roman Empire despite having about as much unity as a bag of cats. Tapestries adorned the walls, sunlight streamed through stained glass windows, and dozens of lords and knights in their finest regalia prepared to hash out yet another land dispute. What they didn't know was that they were literally standing on a disaster waiting to happen.

The meeting had been called by Heinrich VI, the Holy Roman Emperor. This Heinrich was a Hohenstaufen, son of the legendary Frederick Barbarossa, and ruler of territories stretching from the North Sea to the Mediterranean. In an age when most kings struggled to control lands a week's ride from their capitals, Heinrich commanded an empire that spanned modern-day Germany, Austria, parts of Italy, and beyond. He had summoned the assembly to mediate

18

a bitter feud between the Landgrave of Thuringia and the Archbishop of Mainz. These weren't minor squabbles over fence lines, these were the kind of aristocratic grudges that could spiral into civil war if left unchecked. The assembled nobles represented the most powerful families in the German territories, men whose decisions shaped the fate of thousands.

They had chosen to meet in the upper hall of a church building, a suitably grand venue for such important deliberations. What made this particular location less suitable was its position directly above the communal latrine cesspit. Medieval sanitation wasn't exactly cutting-edge technology, and the wooden floor beams supporting the assembly hall had been quietly rotting away above years of accumulated human waste.

When Politics Hit Rock Bottom

The nobles were deep in heated debate when structural physics delivered its own verdict on medieval engineering. With a sound that one contemporary chronicle described as "a great crack and thunderous crash," the entire floor collapsed. In an instant, approximately 60 of Germany's most powerful men plunged two stories straight down into a cesspit filled with what medieval chroniclers delicately referred to as "filth."

The scene was grotesque beyond imagination: armored knights who had survived countless battles now found themselves drowning in sewage, their heavy chainmail dragging them down into depths no warrior should ever have to navigate. Counts and barons who prided themselves on their noble bearing were suddenly flailing in human waste, their elaborate robes and gleaming armor becoming death traps in the most undignified disaster in medieval history. For men who had built their entire identity around honor and dignity, this was a death that stripped away everything they held sacred.

The irony was as thick as the sewage. These were men who had spent their lives literally looking down on the common people, and now they were literally drowning in what those same people had deposited below them. The social hierarchy had been inverted in the most brutal way possible.

Among the victims was Count Heinrich of Schwarzburg and Bishop Dietrich of Meissen. These weren't anonymous peasants, these were men whose deaths would be felt across the empire, their family lines extinguished in a moment of catastrophic plumbing failure.

The Lucky Few

Not everyone shared this fate. King Henry VI himself survived by sheer chance, having been seated in a stone alcove that remained structurally sound while chaos erupted around him. The young king watched in horror as his most important vassals simply vanished through the floor, leaving him clinging to his stone perch until rescuers could lower a ladder.

Archbishop Conrad of Mainz, one of the primary disputants in the original conflict, managed to grab hold of a window ledge and hang there while the disaster unfolded below him. Conrad, drenched in terror and possibly worse, prayed more fervently than he ever had in his life as the sounds of drowning nobles echoed from the pit beneath.

The randomness of survival added another layer of horror to the event. There was no logic to who lived and who died, no correlation between virtue, power, or importance. Fate had sorted the victims with the same arbitrary cruelty as a collapsing floor.

Heinrich VI fled Erfurt immediately after the disaster, understandably traumatized by watching his nobility disappear into a toilet. The dispute he had come to resolve remained unresolved, though one imagines the surviving parties took the event as a rather pointed divine commentary on their quarrel.

The practical aftermath was almost as grim as the disaster itself. Families had to fish their relatives out of the cesspit, a task that transformed noble funeral preparations into something resembling a sewage recovery operation. Medieval chroniclers, usually eager to record the glorious deeds of the aristocracy, found themselves documenting the most undignified deaths in European history.

The political ramifications rippled across the Holy Roman Empire. An entire generation of regional leadership had been wiped out in a single afternoon, leaving power vacuums that would take years to fill. Inheritance disputes exploded as brothers, cousins, and distant relatives suddenly found themselves in line for titles they had never expected to inherit.

The Great Equalizer

What had started as another tedious political assembly ended up resolving the very conflict it was meant to address, just not in the way anyone expected. The main dispute between Landgrave Louis III of Thuringia and Archbishop Conrad of Mainz suddenly seemed trivial after watching dozens of their peers drown in sewage. Louis himself fell into the cesspit but survived, while his primary rival Conrad clung to a latrine chute. The utter horror of the event brought an immediate dose of perspective that no amount of political negotiation could have achieved.

Here were men who commanded armies, owned vast estates, and considered themselves appointed by God to rule over lesser mortals. Yet when the floor gave way, their armor and titles meant nothing. They died exactly as any commoner would have died, drowning in the same human waste that had been deposited by people they would never have acknowledged in life.

Among the victims was Heinrich of Schwarzburg, who according to folk legend had a habit of saying "If I did that, I would have to drown in the privy." The universe, it seems, has a truly dark sense of humor. Count Friedrich I of Abenberg also met his end in the cesspit, proving that fate doesn't discriminate when dispensing ironic justice.

Medieval chroniclers, always eager to find moral lessons in disasters, interpreted the event as divine judgment on pride and worldly ambition. Whether or not God had a hand in the collapse, the disaster certainly demonstrated that no amount of earthly power could exempt you from the basic laws of physics and poor construction.

The tragedy also highlighted the precarious nature of medieval infrastructure. This wasn't a freak accident caused by warfare or natural disaster, this was a building failure that could have been prevented with better engineering. The same society that could construct magnificent cathedrals and imposing castles apparently couldn't figure out how to safely position a meeting hall above a toilet.

Today, the Erfurt latrine disaster is remembered as medieval history's most democratic tragedy. Gravity doesn't care about your title, sewage doesn't respect your noble blood. The nobles had spent their lives concerned with high politics and grand strategy, only to be brought down by the most basic of human necessities. Sometimes, life really does go down the toilet.

Did You Know?

Medieval garderobes often emptied straight down castle walls or into moats below. The streaks of waste actually marked many castle walls for centuries, though the stones survived due to solid construction, not because of any preservative qualities of human waste.

Thomas Crapper didn't invent the flush toilet (that was Sir John Harington in 1596), but he did hold nine patents for toilet improvements and opened the world's first bathroom showroom. Sometimes history's greatest achievement is just having the right surname at the right time.

Roman public toilets had no dividers and featured sponges on sticks called tersorium, rinsed in running water or vinegar between uses. Whether people actually shared these for personal hygiene or just used them to clean the toilets themselves remains debated by historians.

Medieval monks used to share a single towel for drying after washing. It hung on a roller mechanism, when one section got too dirty, they'd roll it to a clean part. Communal hygiene was just how pre-modern life worked, privacy being a luxury few could afford.

The Greedy Cup, Pythagoras' Prank for Fairness

After drowning in chlorine gas and nobles literally drowning in shit, let's lighten things up with a 2,500-year-old practical joke that's still making people laugh today. Sometimes the most enduring inventions are the ones designed to teach greedy people a lesson they'll never forget.

It's around 530 BCE on the Greek island of Samos, and the great mathematician Pythagoras is hosting one of his famous symposiums (ancient Greek drinking parties where scholars would drink wine and debate philosophy). Wine flows freely, philosophical debates rage, and everyone's having a grand time. But there's always that one guy. You know the type – the student who consistently overfills his wine cup while everyone else practices moderation.

Pythagoras watches this behavior with the calculating eye of a man who's spent his life figuring out how the universe works. He disappears into his workshop and emerges with what looks like an ordinary clay cup. He hands it to the greedy student with a sly smile. "Try this one," he suggests.

The student, naturally, fills it to the brim and beyond, determined to get more than his fair share. For a moment, nothing happens. Then, suddenly, the entire contents of the cup drain out through the bottom, soaking his robes and leaving him with absolutely nothing. The room erupts in laughter. Pythagoras has just pulled off history's most educational prank.

When Physics Meets Justice

The Pythagorean cup, also known as the Cup of Justice, is a masterpiece of ancient engineering disguised as a drinking vessel. From the outside, it looks perfectly normal. But hidden inside is a central column with a cleverly designed siphon that turns physics into a moral enforcer.

When you pour wine or water into the cup at a reasonable level, everything functions normally. The liquid stays put, and you can drink to your heart's content. But the moment you get greedy and fill it past a certain line – usually marked by a small ridge inside the cup – physics takes over.

The excess liquid triggers the siphon mechanism. Once the liquid level reaches the top of the hidden tube, it creates a continuous flow that drains the entire cup through a hole in the bottom. One extra drop of greed, and you lose everything. It's like a ancient version of "go directly to jail, do not pass go, do not collect $200," except instead of losing money, you lose your drink and your dignity.

The engineering is elegant in its simplicity. The siphon works on the same principle that drains bathtubs and operates toilet tanks – once you start the flow over the top of the tube, gravity does the rest. No moving parts, no complicated mechanisms, just physics serving justice with a side of humiliation.

The honest answer is probably not. While the cup bears his name and the legend is delightful, Pythagoras was more focused on mathematical theorems and mystical philosophy than designing trick cups. Hero of Alexandria described a similar siphon cup in the 1st century AD, long after Pythagoras had shuffled off this mortal coil. Similar devices popped up throughout medieval Europe, where they were popular party tricks at royal courts.

The name "Pythagorean cup" probably stuck because Pythagoras was famous for his teachings about moderation and balance. He believed "all is number" and that mathematical harmony governed everything from music to morality. "Nothing in excess," he taught his followers, a principle borrowed from the Oracle at Delphi. Whether he invented the cup or not, it embodies his philosophy perfectly. For a man who preached that "the wise man is he who knows the limits of his own ignorance," a device that punishes excess would have been the ultimate teaching tool.

Ancient Wisdom

The cup's lesson remains painfully relevant: take more than your fair share, and you might end up with nothing at all. It's a physical manifestation of the old saying "pigs get fat, hogs get slaughtered," except in this case, hogs get soaked.

The beauty of the Pythagorean cup is that it doesn't rely on honor systems or moral arguments. It simply makes greed self-defeating. There's no negotiating with physics, no appeals to higher authorities, no pleading your case. Fill it too high, and suffer the consequences.

Every time you flush a toilet, you're witnessing the same physics that once soaked greedy Greek students. The toilet tank uses a siphon to create the powerful flush, essentially a Pythagorean cup in reverse.

Walk through the souvenir shops of Crete or Samos today, and you'll find these cups for sale as "Cups of Justice." Tourists inevitably soak themselves while their friends laugh. After 2,500 years, the joke still lands perfectly.

But here's the question: in our modern world of supersized portions and "more is better" mentalities, do we need more Pythagorean cups? Maybe not for wine, but for the things we really overindulge in. The cup reminds us that sometimes the best way to keep what you have is to not reach for more.

Did You Know?

The ancient Roman Emperor Caligula once declared war on Neptune and ordered his soldiers to march to the English Channel and collect seashells as "spoils of victory from the conquered ocean." Like Pythagoras' cup teaching moderation, this was possibly an elaborate prank to humble his arrogant generals - or proof that absolute power makes you absolutely ridiculous.

Benjamin Franklin convinced French aristocrats that bathing was dangerous to their health by claiming Americans stayed clean through "air baths" - sitting naked by open windows. The prank lasted months before anyone realized the inventor of the lightning rod was just mocking European hygiene standards, proving that even brilliant scientists enjoy a good con.

The Last of the Hitler, A Cursed Bloodline

In a modest Long Island suburb in 1973, neighbors knew William Stuart-Houston as the quiet guy who worked at a medical lab and kept his lawn pristine. What they didn't know was that he was burning family photos in his backyard fireplace, systematically erasing evidence that he was born William Patrick Hitler, Adolf's nephew.

The smoke curling into that American autumn carried fragments of a bloodline determined to vanish.

When Soviet artillery shells started landing in the Chancellery garden above his bunker, Adolf Hitler knew the end had come. On April 30, 1945, with Red Army soldiers less than 500 yards away and the sound of Russian boots echoing through Berlin's streets, he put a gun to his head and pulled the trigger. He died childless in that concrete tomb, 50 feet underground.

But the Hitler DNA didn't die with him. It scattered across continents in the bodies of relatives who wanted nothing more than to make it disappear forever. Unlike the conspiracy theories about fleeing Nazis, these relatives weren't heading to Argentina. They were heading toward extinction.

The Nephew Who Fought Back

William Patrick's story reads like dark fiction. Born in Liverpool in 1911 to Adolf's half-brother Alois Jr., he spent his early years trying to capitalize on his famous uncle's rising power. By the 1930s, he was in Germany, asking Uncle Adolf for a better job in the Nazi party.

Adolf reportedly called him his "loathsome nephew."

Smart move by Adolf. By 1938, William Patrick had fled to America and was publicly torching his uncle's reputation. He toured the country giving lectures titled "My Uncle Adolf," then wrote a scathing piece for Look magazine called "Why I Hate My Uncle." Picture the editors' excitement: Hitler's own nephew spilling family secrets in America's most popular magazine.

The article was brutal. William Patrick described Adolf as a volatile, paranoid man who surrounded himself with "a motley crew of the mentally unbalanced." He called the Nazi ideology "a cancer." This wasn't just family gossip, it was a nephew wielding insider knowledge like a scalpel.

Then came the ultimate act of rebellion. In 1944, William Patrick joined the U.S. Navy, serving on a destroyer in the Pacific. The irony was perfect. Hitler's own blood was shooting at Hitler's allies. There's something almost mythological about it, like a Greek tragedy where the family curse turns back on itself.

After the war, William Patrick legally changed his name to Stuart-Houston and disappeared into American suburbia. He married a German war bride named Phyllis, had four sons, and ran a medical laboratory. The American dream, except for the nightmarish surname he'd shed.

The Pact That May Never Have Existed

Sometime in the 1960s, according to persistent rumors, William Patrick and his four sons made a pact. None of them would have children. The Hitler bloodline would end with them.

Alexander Stuart-Houston, one of William's sons, later denied any formal agreement. But he admitted the obvious. None of the brothers married or had kids. Call it coincidence or call it conscience, but the result was the same.

The family silence ran deep. Three brothers became recluses. The fourth, Louis, became a landscape gardener, which seems oddly fitting for someone trying to cultivate a normal life from poisoned soil. The fifth brother, Howard, worked as a Treasury Agent until he died in a car accident in 1989. All remained childless while they lived. All kept their father's adopted name. None spoke publicly about their genetic inheritance.

There's a heartbreaking detail buried in one rare interview. Alexander once revealed he'd been engaged to a Jewish woman. The relationship didn't work out. Here was a man carrying Hitler's DNA, falling in love with someone from the very group his uncle tried to exterminate. History doesn't get more twisted than that. Some names are just too heavy to carry into love.

The Pretenders and Myths

Nature abhors a vacuum, and so does sensational journalism. With the legitimate Hitler line quietly self-destructing, impostors emerged.

Jean-Marie Loret, a Frenchman, spent decades claiming Hitler was his father, allegedly the result of a liaison with his mother during World War I. French tabloids loved it. Historians didn't. DNA tests were inconclusive, and serious scholars dismissed the claim as fantasy. But inconclusive isn't the same as impossible. The truth is, Hitler's movements during WWI are well-documented enough to make such an encounter unlikely, but not entirely beyond the realm of possibility. That sliver of doubt kept the story alive for decades.

Then there was Unity Mitford, the British fascist socialite who supposedly had Hitler's secret love child. The claim rested on her documented infatuation with the Führer and a mysterious pregnancy that ended when she shot herself after Britain declared war on Germany. Another myth that collapsed under scrutiny, but not before spawning countless conspiracy theories. Here, the timeline was even shakier, yet the dramatic elements made it irresistible to conspiracy theorists.

What's fascinating is how these false claims revealed something true about human nature. People desperately wanted Hitler to have had children, as if biological continuation would somehow make his evil more comprehensible or containable. The real descendants, meanwhile, were doing the opposite of what anyone expected. Instead of capitalizing on notoriety or hiding shameful secrets, they were simply trying to live ordinary lives.

The Last Five (Or More)

Today, the count gets complicated. William Patrick died in 1987, taking his secrets with him. His four surviving sons remain: Alexander, Louis, Howard, and Brian Stuart-Houston. They live unremarkable lives in unremarkable places. Alexander worked as a social worker. Louis tends landscapes. The other two stay even further from public view.

But they're not the only ones carrying Hitler's DNA. Two descendants from Adolf's half-sister Angela are still alive: Peter Raubal and Heiner Hochegger. They've managed to stay even more invisible than the Stuart-Houstons, if that's possible.

The math is grim but simple. All these men are elderly, none have children. Adolf Hitler fantasized about a "Thousand-Year Reich" and preached endlessly about Aryan genetic superiority. His own superior genes won't make it to 100 years. The man who obsessed over racial purity and breeding programs couldn't even keep his own bloodline alive for a single century.

When the final Stuart-Houston closes his eyes for the last time, Adolf Hitler's DNA will finally join him in the ground where it belongs. History will remember the name Hitler forever. But biology, thankfully, will not.

Even the name itself has been rejected by the world. Germany, Malaysia, Mexico, and New Zealand have all banned "Adolf Hitler" as a baby name. The most toxic surname in history can't even reproduce itself through adoption.

From Moonshine to Motors, How Prohibition Birthed NASCAR

Appalachian mountains, 1938. A plain-looking 1940 Ford winds through the darkness, its headlights carving narrow beams through mountain fog. To anyone watching, it's just another farm car heading home late. But this Ford carries 180 proof corn liquor in hidden compartments, and beneath its ordinary hood lurks a flathead V8 engine pumped up to over 200 horsepower. When federal headlights appear in the rearview mirror, the driver flips a hidden toggle switch, killing his rear lights, and vanishes into the night like a mechanical ghost.

This wasn't just transportation; it was survival engineering born from one of history's most spectacularly misguided social experiments. The 18th Amendment, passed largely due to the lobbying efforts of the Woman's Christian Temperance Union and the Anti-Saloon League, banned the production and sale of alcoholic beverages in 1920. The reasoning was that alcohol was the root of society's ills: poverty, domestic violence, and moral decay would all disappear if Americans just stopped drinking. What actually happened was that Americans kept drinking but started getting their liquor from criminals instead of legitimate businesses.

The absurdity was profound. A nation that had been built on individual liberty suddenly decided that adults couldn't be trusted to drink responsibly, so the government would make that choice for them. Church groups celebrated the dawn of a new moral age while inadvertently creating the largest criminal enterprise in American history. The same pious reformers who thought they were saving souls instead created a black market that required high-speed chases, mechanical innovation, and driving skills that would have impressed Formula One racers.

In trying to eliminate vice, the temperance movement accidentally invented America's most visceral motorsport. The same churches that had campaigned against demon alcohol had unknowingly laid the foundation for the high-octane spectacle that modern America worships every Sunday afternoon. NASCAR didn't emerge from country clubs or racing academies; it was born in the hollers of Appalachia, where necessity taught ordinary men to build extraordinary machines and desperation made them drive those machines faster than anyone thought possible.

Sports history is littered with similar accidents of invention. Basketball was created because a YMCA instructor needed an indoor winter activity for his students. Volleyball emerged when another YMCA director found basketball too strenuous for older members. Golf supposedly began when Scottish shepherds started hitting stones into rabbit holes with their walking sticks. NASCAR's origin story stands apart in its uniquely American contradiction. A sport built on speed and rebellion, created by a moral crusade that tried to eliminate both.

Economics 101: The Moonshine Market

Welcome to the most practical economics lesson in American history. When the government eliminated the legal supply of alcohol in 1920, demand remained exactly where it had always been, everywhere. Alcohol is what economists call an inelastic good, meaning people will pay almost any price to get it and consumption barely changes regardless of cost or legal status. Basic economic theory predicted what would happen next, prices would rise, profit margins would skyrocket, and entrepreneurs would emerge to fill the gap. What the theory books didn't mention was that these entrepreneurs would need to outrun federal agents while carrying 400-pound loads of corn liquor through mountain passes at midnight.

The moonshine business operated on simple principles that would have made Adam Smith proud. High demand, limited supply, enormous profit margins, and the kind of barriers to entry that kept out casual competitors. The main barrier wasn't capital or expertise; it was the willingness to risk federal prison while driving a heavily modified automobile at dangerous speeds through terrain that would challenge a mountain goat.

Mountain communities that had been quietly distilling corn liquor for generations suddenly found themselves operating in what economists call a "high-velocity market." The faster you could move product from production to consumption, the higher your profit margins and the lower your chance of meeting federal enforcement. Speed wasn't just an advantage; it was the entire business model.

This created what might be called "performance economics." Every modification to a bootlegger's car was a business investment designed to increase revenue per mile. Stiffer rear suspensions weren't automotive enthusiast upgrades; they were load-bearing solutions for an industry where payload capacity directly determined profit potential. A typical moonshine load weighed 400-500 pounds, enough to make any stock suspension obvious to observant federal agents. The solution was engineering disguised as mechanical necessity: heavy-duty truck springs replaced standard leaf springs, second axles distributed weight evenly, and custom shock absorbers kept cars level under illegal loads.

The engine modifications represented pure return-on-investment calculations. Bootleggers favored Ford's flathead V8 not for brand loyalty but for cost-effectiveness: parts were cheap, modifications were straightforward, and the basic architecture could handle significant performance upgrades. A stock flathead produced about 85 horsepower, perfectly adequate for legitimate transportation but insufficient for high-speed federal evasion. Multiple carburetors, high-compression cylinder heads, and custom intake manifolds transformed family sedans into mechanical outlaws capable of outrunning anything the government could afford.

The aesthetic was crucial to the business model. These cars had to look like grocery-getters while performing like rockets. Junior Johnson's famous 1940 Ford served double duty: hauling illegal liquor on Saturday nights and appearing respectably ordinary at Sunday church services. The dents from dodging roadblocks became Monday morning conversation pieces, though their origins remained professionally confidential until decades after the statute of limitations expired.

The tactical innovations would have impressed military strategists. Hidden toggle switches killed rear lights, letting drivers vanish around curves while agents chased phantom tail lights. The "blocker" car system operated as corporate sacrifice: expendable vehicles deliberately engaged federal agents while primary loads escaped through alternate routes. Risk management at 90 miles per hour.

From Outlaw to Folk Hero

Picture Junior Johnson on a moonless night in 1955, hunched over the wheel of his 1940 Ford as headlights appeared in his rearview mirror. The car behind him carried 400 pounds of white lightning, and Johnson knew that staying close would make both vehicles appear as a single set of tail lights to any federal agents watching from a distance. He had discovered drafting not through wind tunnel testing but through desperation, learning that two cars running nose-to-tail could disappear into the night like a mechanical ghost train.

The technique that would later make him a NASCAR legend was born from pure survival instinct. Johnson would tuck his Ford so close behind another bootlegger's car that their bumpers nearly touched, both drivers maintaining 80 miles per hour through mountain curves where a single mistake meant either federal prison or a fiery crash into Appalachian granite. The aerodynamic benefit was accidental; the invisibility was intentional.

When federal roadblocks appeared ahead, Johnson deployed what became known as the "bootleg turn." Picture the physics: steering wheel yanked hard left while simultaneously slamming the handbrake and flooring the accelerator. The Ford would spin 180 degrees in a cloud of burning rubber and gravel, its momentum carrying it backward down the mountain road before Johnson could shift into reverse and disappear into the darkness. Federal agents would scramble from their positions expecting to arrest a trapped criminal, only to find empty road and the fading sound of a flathead V8 engine echoing through the hollers.

The revenuers weren't amateur hour. Agent Joe Carter, working the North Carolina mountains in the 1950s, carried a radio that could coordinate roadblocks across three counties. His team deployed spike strips made from welded railroad spikes, devices that could shred tires at 60 miles per hour and send bootleggers tumbling into ravines. They drove souped-up government Fords that could hit 100 miles per hour on straightaways, and they knew the mountain roads almost as well as the men they were chasing.

This arms race created a unique form of mechanical evolution. Johnson learned to read road surface through steering wheel vibrations, distinguishing between loose gravel that would provide traction for emergency turns and packed dirt that would cause fatal slides. He could navigate by engine sound alone, using the echo off mountain walls to judge his distance from cliff edges on roads where headlights would betray his position to federal agents positioned miles away.

The stakes made every skill life-or-death essential. A bootlegger who couldn't maintain control while carrying 400 pounds of sloshing corn liquor at dangerous speeds would find his family facing starvation while he served five years in federal prison. Johnson once drove 47 miles through the Blue Ridge Mountains with a blown rear tire, using nothing but throttle control and prayer to keep his Ford upright while agents pursued him through switchback curves that would challenge a mountain goat.

These weren't showboat maneuvers performed for impressed spectators. They were survival techniques developed by men who understood that mechanical failure or driving error meant the difference between feeding their children and watching them grow up through prison visiting room glass. Every bootleg turn, every high-speed chase, every midnight run through mountain passes was a graduate course in automotive performance taught by necessity and graded by federal agents with handcuffs.

The Great Legitimization

By the 1930s, bootleggers had created an underground culture of mechanical innovation and driving excellence that was too entertaining to ignore. Local communities began organizing informal races where these modified cars could compete legally. Dirt tracks sprouted across the rural South, initially as informal gatherings but gradually evolving into organized events that drew substantial crowds.

The Daytona Beach and Road Course became the crown jewel of this emerging sport. The 4.1-mile track combined hard-packed beach sand with parallel asphalt highway, creating a venue where bootleggers' souped-up cars could reach speeds that would have been impossible on conventional dirt tracks. The beach setting added spectacle to competition, with cars racing past sunbathers and tourists who stopped to watch ordinary-looking automobiles achieve extraordinary speeds.

These races weren't just entertainment; they became crucial components of local economies. Farmers, mechanics, and townspeople gathered not only to watch but to socialize, trade, and place bets. The events provided legal outlets for engineering and driving skills that had been perfected in shadows, while generating revenue for communities that had few other sources of outside income.

The transition from crime to sport revealed the bootleggers' true innovation. Their mechanical modifications, developed to evade federal agents, proved superior to anything conventional automotive manufacturers were producing. Their driving techniques, learned through life-or-death necessity, made them natural competitors in organized racing. The same men who had been federal fugitives on Saturday night became local heroes on Sunday afternoon.

Bill France's Masterstroke

Bill France Sr. recognized that this chaotic collection of local races and outlaw drivers represented untapped commercial potential. In December 1947, he called a meeting at the Streamline Hotel in Daytona Beach that would formalize the transition from bootlegging to big business. The gathering included drivers, mechanics, and promoters who had been operating independently across the South.

France's genius lay in understanding that structure could enhance rather than diminish the sport's outlaw appeal. He established uniform rules that made competition fair while preserving the mechanical innovation that made it exciting. The points system he created turned individual races into season-long championships, giving fans ongoing narrative investment. Most importantly, he legitimized skills that had previously been criminal liabilities.

The National Association for Stock Car Auto Racing, founded in 1948, represented more than organizational efficiency; it was cultural alchemy. France transformed illegal activity into legal entertainment, criminal fugitives into celebrated athletes, and underground economy into mainstream business.

The same driving skills that had once meant federal prosecution now generated fan adoration and commercial sponsorship.

Junior Johnson's career trajectory illustrates this transformation perfectly. The man who had dodged federal agents through Appalachian mountains became a NASCAR champion who was celebrated for the same abilities that had once made him a wanted criminal. His 1965 Sports Illustrated profile described him as "The Last American Hero," cementing his transition from outlaw to icon.

Sunday School Speedway

NASCAR's current status as America's second most popular sport traces directly to Prohibition-era necessity. The same mechanical innovations that helped moonshiners evade federal agents now help drivers win races worth millions of dollars. The driving techniques developed on midnight runs through mountain roads are now studied by professional racing teams with sophisticated technical resources.

The sport's appeal stems partly from this authentic outlaw heritage. NASCAR didn't emerge from elite racing traditions or expensive technical academies; it grew from working-class ingenuity applied to illegal enterprise. Modern fans understand instinctively that the skills they're watching were forged by necessity rather than taught by instructors.

The cultural irony is profound: America's most popular motorsport celebrates precisely the kind of law-breaking that contemporary society condemns. Modern NASCAR drivers are honored for possessing skills that their predecessors developed while committing federal crimes. The sport's marketing emphasizes rebellion and independence while operating within thoroughly regulated legal frameworks.

Perhaps most remarkably, NASCAR's success vindicated the bootleggers' original innovation. Their mechanical modifications, dismissed by legitimate automotive manufacturers as crude backyard tinkering, proved superior to factory engineering. Their driving techniques, learned through desperate necessity, established standards that professional drivers still struggle to match.

The moonshine runners of Prohibition era created more than fast cars and daring escapes; they established a template for American automotive culture that persists today. Every modified car, every amateur racing event, every driver who pushes a machine beyond its intended limits carries forward traditions established by men who needed to outrun federal agents to feed their families. The bootleggers may have lost the war against Prohibition, but their mechanical legacy won something more lasting: America's automotive soul.

Did You Know?

Junior Johnson discovered drafting could save 20% on fuel consumption. NASCAR tried to ban it until they realized it made races more exciting. Sometimes the best innovations are the ones you can't stop.

Lightning Moonshine, legal Tennessee whiskey, is now sold at NASCAR races. The sport that began with illegal liquor runners now officially serves the same recipe their founders were smuggling. Corporate sponsorship comes full circle.

Modern NASCAR pit crews can change four tires and refuel in under 12 seconds, faster than most people can parallel park. These athletes train like Navy SEALs, because at 200 mph, every second costs positions.

From Bloodshed to Benevolence, The Emperor's Redemption

In 261 BCE, Emperor Ashoka of India stood on the Kalinga battlefield surveying a scene that would make Quentin Tarantino take notes. Blood soaked the earth so thoroughly that the nearby river had been rebranded as the Ganges Red. A hundred thousand corpses littered the ground, and the air hung thick with smoke and the metallic stench of death. For most conquerors, this would have been another successful quarterly review. For Ashoka, it became his road to Damascus moment.

The emperor who had earned the charming nickname "Chandashoka" (Ashoka the Fierce) suddenly found himself having what can only be described as history's most expensive therapy session. Here was a man who had once executed 500 ministers over a workplace disagreement, burned his concubines alive in a fit of rage, and generally treated human life like office supplies. Yet standing there among the carnage, something inside him snapped. Or perhaps, for the first time in his life, something finally clicked.

How to Win Friends and Incinerate People

Before his battlefield epiphany, Ashoka had been the kind of ruler who made Caligula look reasonable. But he hadn't started out expecting the crown. As the third son of Emperor Bindusara, Ashoka was originally meant to be the family spare, like a royal understudy destined for a quiet life of provincial governorship while his older brother Susima inherited the empire. Unfortunately for everyone involved, Ashoka had other plans.

Part of the problem was that Ashoka had always been the black sheep of the royal family. His mother, Subhadrangi, was a commoner from the merchant class, a barber's daughter who had caught the emperor's eye but never his full respect. In a court obsessed with bloodline purity, this made Ashoka something of an embarrassment to his father. Bindusara reportedly called his son "Ashoka the Unpleasant," a nickname that must have stung given that "Ashoka" literally means "without sorrow." The irony was brutal: a prince named "joyful" who brought his father nothing but disappointment.

Unlike his full-blooded royal half-brothers, Ashoka had to prove himself through competence rather than birthright. This drove him to excel in military matters and administration, but it also bred a ruthless ambition that his father found troubling. Bindusara seemed to sense something dangerous in his third son, a hunger that went beyond normal royal ambition. The emperor's preference for Susima wasn't just about birth order, it was about character. He saw in Ashoka a darkness that made him unsuitable for the throne.

The succession crisis began when Bindusara fell gravely ill around 273 BCE. According to Buddhist sources, Susima was away governing the western provinces when their father's health declined, leaving a power vacuum that Ashoka was quick to exploit. He had been serving as viceroy of Ujjain, where he'd already demonstrated his administrative ruthlessness and military competence. More crucially, he had cultivated relationships with key ministers and generals in the capital, understanding that in a court that looked down on his mixed heritage, loyalty would have to be bought rather than inherited.

When news of Bindusara's deteriorating condition reached the court, Ashoka moved swiftly. He returned to Pataliputra and began consolidating power while his brothers were scattered across the empire's vast territories. The ancient sources suggest he used a combination of political maneuvering and outright violence to eliminate potential rivals. He allegedly killed 99 of his half-brothers to secure the throne, methodically hunting down anyone with a legitimate claim to succession.

The scale of the fratricide was breathtaking even by ancient standards. Ashoka didn't just eliminate immediate threats, he conducted what amounted to a systematic purge of the royal bloodline. The only brother he spared was Tissa, whom he apparently found useful, possibly as a loyal administrator who posed no political threat. Some sources suggest Tissa may have actively supported Ashoka's coup, choosing survival over principle.

The succession war lasted nearly four years, from 273 to 269 BCE, as Ashoka fought to establish his legitimacy against various claimants and rebellious governors. He faced resistance not just from surviving family members but from nobles who questioned his right to rule. The violence was so extensive that later Buddhist texts, despite their reverence for the reformed Ashoka, couldn't completely whitewash this blood-soaked origin story. Even by ancient Indian standards, where royal fratricide was practically a coming-of-age ritual, Ashoka's methods were considered excessive.

Once crowned, the legends paint him as a sadist who delighted in creative punishments, maintaining elaborate torture chambers, and treating his subjects like chess pieces in a very bloody game. He allegedly built a prison so horrific that visitors mistook it for hell itself, complete with a staff that specialized in keeping people alive just long enough to regret it. The man had serious anger management issues, but then again, when you've murdered most of your family for a job, workplace stress takes on new dimensions.

But here's the thing about absolute power in ancient times: if you were an emperor having a bad day, entire cities could pay the price. Ashoka's early reign was what happens when you give war elephants to someone with daddy issues.

The War That Broke the Warlord

The Kalinga War wasn't just another military campaign for Ashoka. It was his magnum opus, the violent crescendo of a career built on conquest. By 262 BCE, he had already unified most of India under the Mauryan Empire—his grandfather's creation that stretched from Afghanistan to Bangladesh. But one significant piece remained stubbornly independent: Kalinga.

This wasn't some minor holdout province. Kalinga encompassed what is now the state of Odisha, plus parts of northern Andhra Pradesh and southern West Bengal, controlling crucial ports along the Bay of Bengal and the trade routes between northern and southern India. It was strategically vital, economically prosperous, and militarily formidable. For Ashoka, it represented the one puzzle piece missing from his imperial collection, and like any obsessive collector, he had to have it.

The war itself was brutal even by ancient standards. Ashoka mobilized massive forces, deploying war elephants, cavalry, and hundreds of thousands of infantry across a front that spanned hundreds of miles of difficult terrain, from coastal plains to dense forests to river deltas. The Kalinga forces, fighting for their homeland's independence, offered fierce resistance. The fighting was so intense that Greek ambassadors who witnessed it described scenes that wouldn't be out of place in the Iliad. When the dust settled across what is now eastern India, 100,000 Kalinga soldiers lay dead, 150,000 had been deported, and countless civilians had perished from disease and famine.

But victory felt different this time. Perhaps it was seeing a Kalinga mother weeping over her child's body in the ruins of what is now Bhubaneswar. Perhaps it was walking through streets where dogs feasted on human remains. Perhaps it was simply the accumulated weight of decades of violence finally crushing whatever remained of his conscience. Whatever the trigger, Ashoka experienced something that would be familiar to anyone who has ever looked in the mirror after a particularly ugly breakup: the sudden, horrifying realization that he might be the villain in this story.

Stone Cold Remorse

What happened next was remarkable even by the standards of ancient history. Ashoka didn't just feel bad about the war, he carved his remorse into stone for posterity. His Rock Edict 13 reads like a public apology letter written by someone who genuinely understands the magnitude of his mistakes. "The slaughter, death, and carrying away captive that takes place when a country unconquered is being conquered is a matter of profound sorrow and regret to His Sacred Majesty," he wrote.

But this wasn't an overnight Damascus-road conversion. Ashoka's embrace of Buddhism unfolded like a carefully orchestrated campaign. Buddhism, barely three centuries old at the time, offered something radically different from the violent Hinduism of his upbringing: a path to enlightenment through compassion, non-violence, and the elimination of suffering. The Buddha's core teaching that all suffering comes from human desire and attachment must have resonated with an emperor who had just witnessed the ultimate cost of his own territorial ambitions.

He first approached the faith as a lay disciple, dipping his toes in Buddhist waters while still maintaining the imperial lifestyle. Only later, under the influence of a persuasive Buddhist monk, did he fully commit to promoting the religion's principles of ahimsa (non-violence). It was spiritual transformation by installments, the ancient equivalent of a gradual lifestyle rebrand.

His communication strategy was revolutionary for its time. Rather than simply issuing decrees from his palace, Ashoka pioneered what might be called history's first multilingual public relations campaign. His edicts weren't carved in a single imperial tongue but appeared in Prakrit, Greek, and Aramaic, ensuring his message of moral reform could be understood across his linguistically diverse empire. He employed multiple scripts including Brahmi and Kharoshthi, creating a sophisticated network of stone-carved messaging that reached from Afghanistan to southern India. These weren't just royal proclamations, they were carefully crafted attempts to speak directly to his subjects in their own languages about his transformed worldview.

This wasn't just ancient spin control. Ashoka backed up his words with a complete overhaul of his governance philosophy. He began treating his subjects not as property but as his "children." The emperor who had once measured success in body counts now measured it in wells dug and hospitals built.

The transformation earned him a new nickname: "Dharmashoka" (the Righteous Ashoka). He established hospitals for both humans and animals, planted shade trees along dusty roads, dug wells in remote villages, and sent Buddhist missionaries across Asia like ancient peace corps volunteers. He even gave up hunting, which for an ancient Indian king was like giving up breathing. The man who once found entertainment in elaborate executions now spent his time building rest houses for weary travelers.

The Ancient Art of Damage Control

Of course, not everyone buys the complete saint narrative. Some historians argue that the legends of both his early cruelty and later sainthood were exaggerated over time, like a very ancient version of telephone. After all, every good redemption story needs a properly villainous beginning.

There's also the practical consideration that proclaiming yourself reformed after conquering most of a continent is excellent PR. Nothing says "legitimate ruler" quite like carved stone monuments explaining how sorry you are about all that conquering. Ashoka might have been genuinely remorseful, but he was also politically savvy enough to understand that ruling through fear only works until someone scarier comes along.

Here's what gets overlooked: Ashoka never actually gave up being emperor. He kept his armies, his tax collectors, and his conquered territories. He just ruled with compassion instead of pure fear. It was the same iron fist, now wearing a velvet glove.

This wasn't hypocrisy, it was survival. Ashoka understood that in a world of rival kingdoms, unilateral disarmament meant death. His conversion changed his methods, not his grip on power.

When Good Emperors Go Bad (Again)

Ashoka's impact on world history is undeniable. His missionaries spread Buddhism from Afghanistan to Sri Lanka, reshaping Asia's spiritual landscape. His multilingual edicts represent some of the earliest examples of state-sponsored moral philosophy. He invented the concept of governmental responsibility for citizens' welfare, an idea that wouldn't resurface in the West for another thousand years.

When Britain finally left India in 1947, the new nation needed a flag. They could have chosen any symbol for the center of their tricolor. Instead, they picked the Ashoka Chakra, a 2,000-year-old wheel representing righteousness and law. So every time India's flag flies, it's celebrating a symbol created by a man who slaughtered his way to power, then spent the rest of his life trying to atone for it.

But personal transformation couldn't fix everything. After his death, his sons fought viciously for power, and his massive infrastructure projects had stretched the treasury to breaking point. The hospitals and roads that demonstrated his compassion became financial anchors dragging the empire toward bankruptcy. Without his unifying presence, the realm fractured, the dead of Kalinga remained dead, and the cycle of violence continued. Yet his stone pillars still dot India, their inscriptions worn smooth by centuries of weather. The emperor who once measured success in body counts left behind proof that even the most corrupted individuals can change, even if they can't undo their past.

Did You Know?

Modern India's national emblem features four lions from Ashoka's pillars, but the original also had a bull and horse that got edited out. Even ancient symbols need good graphic design.

Ashoka banned animal sacrifice across his empire but made exceptions for his kitchen staff. Apparently moral reformation has to be practical, you can't run an empire on vegetables alone when you're feeding half a million soldiers.

The Kalinga War generated so many refugees that it created India's first humanitarian crisis. Ashoka's response was to invent disaster relief, complete with organized food distribution and temporary housing.

Ashoka's stone edicts were the world's first multilingual government PR campaign, appearing in Greek, Aramaic, and local languages. He basically invented the press release 2,300 years before anyone thought to call it that.

The Mauryan Empire had a postal system so efficient that messages could travel from Afghanistan to Bangladesh faster than most modern bureaucracies process paperwork. Ancient Indians figured out logistics while Europe was still arguing about which end of a sword to hold.

Buddhist monks were the world's first international consultants, traveling thousands of miles to advise kings on everything from irrigation to moral philosophy. They charged nothing but rice and enlightenment.

Hysteria in Salem, When Neighbors Became Witches

In the autumn of 1692, Salem Village looked like a postcard from Puritan paradise. Maple trees blazed orange and red, harvest corn stood in neat rows, and church bells rang out over tidy cottages where God-fearing families prepared for another New England winter. Then the screaming started.

It began in the parsonage of Reverend Samuel Parris, where his nine-year-old daughter Betty and eleven-year-old niece Abigail Williams started having what can only be described as the world's first recorded case of collective teenage drama. The girls writhed on the floor, barked like dogs, complained of invisible pinching, and claimed they were being tormented by specters only they could see. In a community where a crooked fence post could spark a property dispute lasting decades, the girls' supernatural afflictions were about to unleash something far worse than any demon: human nature itself.

The Teenage Witch Hunters

What happened next would make mean girls everywhere take notes. Betty Parris and Abigail Williams had stumbled upon the ultimate power move in a society that normally treated children like furniture. In Puritan Salem, girls their age were expected to be seen and not heard, to spend their days spinning wool and memorizing Bible verses. But writhe around screaming about witches? Suddenly every adult in the village hung on their every word.

The performance was intoxicating. When local doctor William Griggs examined the girls and found no physical cause for their fits, he delivered the diagnosis that would change everything: "The evil hand is upon them." Within weeks, more girls joined the act. Ann Putnam Jr., Mary Walcott, and Mercy Lewis all began experiencing similar "torments," creating what amounted to Salem's first girl gang.

The psychology was brilliant in its simplicity. These girls had discovered that in a world where they had no power, claiming to be victims of supernatural assault gave them the ultimate authority. Who would dare contradict a child possessed by demons? Their word became law, their pointing fingers became death sentences, and their teenage tantrums became matters of eternal salvation.

The first victims were predictable: social outcasts who couldn't fight back. Sarah Good was a homeless beggar who went door to door asking for food. Sarah Osborne hadn't attended church in over a year and had scandalized the community by living with a man before marrying him. Tituba, Reverend Parris's enslaved woman from Barbados, was foreign and practiced what the Puritans considered heathen customs. These women were already on the margins of society, making them perfect scapegoats for whatever was ailing Salem's suddenly possessed children.

But the girls' accusations quickly revealed that this wasn't random supernatural targeting. It was strategic social warfare with a body count.

When Property Lines Become Battle Lines

Salem Village in 1692 was less a community than a collection of barely contained feuds wrapped in Puritan piety. The most bitter rivalry pitted the Putnam family against nearly everyone else, but especially the Porter clan and anyone associated with Salem Town, the more prosperous coastal settlement that Salem Village resented for its wealth and worldliness.

The Putnams were Salem Village royalty, or at least they thought they should be. They owned vast tracts of land, held prominent positions in the church, and had been feuding with their neighbors over everything from property boundaries to pig ownership since the day they arrived. Thomas Putnam Jr. was particularly litigious, a man who seemed to view every sunrise as an opportunity to file a new lawsuit against someone.

When his daughter Ann Putnam Jr. began naming witches, the family connections were impossible to ignore. Nearly every person she accused had somehow crossed the Putnam family. The Nurses had disputed land boundaries. The Proctors had opposed Reverend Parris's appointment. The Coreys had testified against Putnam interests in court. It was as if Ann had weaponized her supernatural visions to settle her father's grudges.

The masterstroke came when Ann accused Rebecca Nurse, a seventy-year-old grandmother so beloved that even her enemies respected her piety. Rebecca's family had been locked in a decades-long dispute with the Putnams over a tract of land that both families claimed. When Ann pointed her finger at Rebecca and screamed that the old woman's specter was tormenting her, it became clear that in Salem, witchcraft accusations were just property disputes by other means.

The genius of it was that supernatural claims couldn't be cross-examined. How do you defend against charges that your invisible spirit attacked someone in their dreams? The Putnams had found the perfect weapon: teenage girls whose visions conveniently aligned with their family's enemies list.

The Ergot Factor

Here's where the story takes a turn into accidental pharmacology. Some modern scientists have suggested that Salem's witch crisis might have had a chemical cause: ergot poisoning from contaminated rye grain. Ergot is a fungus that grows on rye and contains alkaloids similar to LSD. In the right conditions, eating ergot-contaminated bread can cause hallucinations, seizures, and a burning sensation in the limbs that victims described as feeling like they were on fire.

The theory is tantalizing. Salem had experienced an unusually wet spring and summer in 1691, perfect conditions for ergot growth. The symptoms the afflicted girls described, convulsions and the sensation of being pinched and bitten, match ergot poisoning. Even more intriguingly, the accusations stopped coming from the western, swampy part of Salem Village (where ergot would thrive) and shifted to the drier eastern section as the trials progressed.

It's possible that Salem's witch hunt was history's first documented bad trip. Picture Puritan families sitting down to their evening bread, unknowingly ingesting a fungus that would make them see demons dancing on their dinner tables. In a community already primed to believe in supernatural evil, ergot-induced hallucinations would have seemed like proof positive that the Devil had come to Massachusetts.

The theory isn't proven, and it doesn't explain why only certain people were affected or why the accusations followed such predictable social patterns. But it adds a darkly comic twist to the Salem story: what if the real witch was in the bread box all along?

Courtroom Theater

The Salem witch trials represented justice at its most theatrical and logic at its most absent. The court operated under special rules that would have made Alice in Wonderland's Queen of Hearts proud. "Spectral evidence" was not only admissible but often the primary proof of guilt. If an accuser claimed to see the defendant's specter tormenting them, that was enough for a conviction.

But spectral evidence wasn't the only absurd "proof" the court accepted. They also employed the "touch test," a piece of judicial logic so twisted it could only have been invented by people who had clearly never heard of coincidence. If an accuser was writhing in a fit, the accused witch would be ordered to touch them. If the victim's convulsions suddenly stopped, it was considered ironclad proof that the accused was indeed the source of their torment. It was like a supernatural version of "whoever smelt it, dealt it," except with death sentences.

The Court of Oyer and Terminer was presided over by men with no legal training whatsoever. Chief Justice William Stoughton had never practiced law, yet somehow found himself determining matters of life and death based on whether invisible birds were perching on people's shoulders. There were no defense attorneys, no cross-examination of accusers, and no adherence to English common law. It was less a court than a theater where the outcome was predetermined and the only question was how dramatically the accused would be condemned.

The trials revealed the terrifying power of mass hysteria amplified by official incompetence. When respected judges nodded solemnly as teenage girls claimed to be pinched by invisible specters, it legitimized madness and made rational people question their own sanity. If the courts said spectral evidence was real, who were ordinary citizens to disagree?

Perhaps most chilling was how quickly neighbors turned on each other. People who had shared Sunday dinners suddenly testified about suspicious behaviors they claimed to have noticed years earlier. A woman's failure to cry at her child's funeral became evidence of witchcraft. A man's success with his crops suggested a demonic bargain. In Salem, being different, successful, or simply disliked became potentially fatal.

The accused faced an impossible choice. Confess to witchcraft and live (but be forever branded as a servant of Satan), or maintain your innocence and hang. Most chose the gallows over the lie. But one man, 80-year-old Giles Corey, found a third option that was somehow even worse.

When Corey refused to enter any plea at all, the court decided to persuade him through peine forte et dure, "strong and hard punishment." They placed a wooden board on his chest and began piling stones on top, slowly crushing him to extract a confession. For two days, as the weight increased, Corey's only response was "More weight." He died without entering a plea, which meant the government couldn't confiscate his property. His estate went to his children instead of the crown. It was a final act of defiance that cost him everything but saved his family's future.

The Tipping Point

The witch hunt might have continued indefinitely if not for a classic case of political overreach. In September 1692, the afflicted girls made their biggest mistake: they accused Lady Mary Phips, wife of Massachusetts Governor William Phips, of witchcraft.

Suddenly, spectral evidence didn't seem quite so reliable. Governor Phips, who had been traveling when the trials began, returned to find his wife among the accused and his colony in chaos. With the speed of a man whose spouse had just been branded a servant of Satan, he dissolved the special court and banned the use of spectral evidence in future trials.

It was a perfect illustration of how hysteria ends: not with enlightenment or justice, but when powerful people finally feel threatened. The same evidence that had condemned twenty people to death suddenly became inadmissible when it targeted the governor's wife. The witch hunt that had torn Salem apart stopped not because people came to their senses, but because the wrong person got accused.

The Reckoning

By 1693, the fever had broken. Many of the accusers, including Ann Putnam Jr., eventually confessed they had fabricated their stories. In 1706, Ann stood before Salem Village's congregation and asked for forgiveness, admitting she had been "deluded by Satan" into making false accusations. It was the closest thing to justice the victims would receive during their lifetimes.

But the scope of Salem's madness becomes even more disturbing when you consider its victims. The youngest person accused was four-year-old Dorothy Good, daughter of the already condemned Sarah Good. Magistrates questioned this preschooler about her alleged witchcraft, coerced a confession from her tiny lips, and threw her in prison for eight months. While Dorothy sat in a colonial jail cell, her mother was hanged. The trauma left Dorothy mentally damaged for life. Nothing quite captures the insanity of Salem like the image of grown men interrogating a toddler about her supernatural crimes.

The Massachusetts General Court eventually annulled the convictions and paid restitution to the victims' families. But the damage was done. Salem had proven that a community could literally consume itself when fear overrode reason and neighbor turned against neighbor.

What makes Salem's story particularly American is how small-scale and late it was compared to the European witch hunts. While tens of thousands died as witches across Europe over several centuries, Salem's hysteria killed twenty people in less than a year. The trials occurred just as Europe's "witch craze" was winding down, making Salem something of a historical footnote that became outsized in American memory. Perhaps that's fitting for a young nation that would later excel at turning local scandals into national obsessions.

Today, Salem has embraced its dark history with the enthusiasm of a town that discovered trauma could be monetized. Tourists buy witch-themed merchandise and pose with costumed actors pretending to cast spells. There's something fitting about a place where twenty people died for allegedly practicing witchcraft now celebrating Halloween year-round.

Because Salem's witch trials were never really about witchcraft. They were about the same things that fuel every modern panic: property disputes, teenage attention-seeking, and neighbors settling scores. The real magic was how ordinary human spite transformed a quiet farming village into America's template for mass hysteria.

The victims were finally exonerated in 2001, more than 300 years later. But perhaps the most chilling detail remains four-year-old Dorothy Good, questioned by magistrates about her supernatural crimes and imprisoned for eight months while her mother hanged. In Salem, even the children weren't safe from adult madness. The witches were never the real threat. The real danger was neighbors with grudges and the power to make them stick.

Did You Know?

The "Great Fear" of 1789 spread across France faster than actual news could travel, with peasants in villages hundreds of miles apart simultaneously becoming convinced that brigands were coming to destroy their crops. Like Salem's teenage accusers, French peasants turned their terror into targeted attacks on their social enemies - burning manor houses instead of hanging neighbors.

The Dancing Plague of 1518 killed more people than some medieval battles, except the weapons were exhaustion and dehydration instead of swords. Strasbourg authorities made the same mistake as Salem's judges - they took the madness seriously and made it worse by hiring musicians and building stages for the dancers.

The Lodestone's Secret, How the Compass Found North

Around 200 BCE, a fortune-teller stood before China's imperial court. The Han Dynasty, one of ancient China's most powerful ruling families, controlled a vast empire. The fortune-teller placed a curious spoon-shaped piece of lodestone on a polished bronze plate. The assembled nobles watched in hushed amazement as the spoon slowly rotated. Its handle pointed south as if pulled by an invisible hand. They thought they were witnessing magic. They were actually seeing the world's first compass. It would take nearly a thousand years before anyone thought to take this mystical divination tool to sea.

The lodestone spoon was used for feng shui, the Chinese practice of arranging buildings and objects to create good luck and harmony, helping emperors position their palaces and tombs in harmony with cosmic forces. For centuries, it remained a tool of fortune-tellers and geomancers, people who claimed they could predict the future by reading the earth and magnetic forces. Its true potential lay locked away in superstition and ceremony. But the needle that would eventually guide Columbus to the New World was already spinning in that bronze dish, waiting for someone to realize its revolutionary secret.

From Fortune-Telling to Sea-Faring

The breakthrough came during the Song Dynasty, when Chinese scholars began to understand that lodestone's mysterious power could serve more practical purposes than reading fortunes. Shen Kuo, a brilliant polymath writing in 1088, became the first person to explicitly describe using a magnetized needle for navigation rather than divination.

Shen's innovation was elegantly simple. Rub an iron needle against lodestone until it becomes magnetized, then float it on water or suspend it on a silk thread. The needle would consistently point toward magnetic north, providing a reliable reference direction regardless of weather, time of day, or celestial visibility. What had been a parlor trick for court mystics became a lifeline for sailors.

By 1117, Chinese maritime records show that sea captains were routinely using "south-pointing fish," compass needles shaped like fish floating in water bowls. These early compasses freed Chinese sailors from their dependence on clear skies and familiar coastlines. Navigation in fog, storms, or the open ocean became possible. Ships could venture farther from land with confidence, knowing they could always find their way home.

The psychological impact was as important as the practical one. For millennia, sailors had been at the mercy of the elements, praying for clear skies to reveal the stars they needed for navigation. The compass gave them power over uncertainty, transforming the trackless ocean into a navigable highway marked by an invisible magnetic road.

The Knowledge Travels West

The compass didn't stay in China long. By the late 12th century, Arab traders sailing the Indian Ocean had discovered this remarkable Chinese invention and brought it westward. The knowledge traveled along the same maritime trade routes that carried silk, spices, and porcelain, spreading through the Islamic world and eventually reaching Mediterranean ports.

The first European mention comes from Alexander Neckam, an English scholar who noted around 1190 that sailors were using magnetized needles to find their direction when stars were hidden. European mariners, who had relied on primitive methods like following bird flights and reading wave patterns, had access to a tool that seemed almost supernatural in its reliability.

Italian merchants, always quick to adopt innovations that could improve their profitable Mediterranean trade, were among the first Europeans to embrace the compass enthusiastically. They refined the design, mounting needles on pivots and adding compass roses marked with direction points. These improvements made the compass more accurate and easier to read, especially in rough seas.

The compass spread rapidly across cultures. Unlike many technological innovations that required extensive explanation or cultural adaptation, the compass was immediately comprehensible. Point the needle north, sail in any direction with confidence.

The Age of Discovery Begins

The compass didn't just improve navigation; it enabled exploration on a scale previously unimaginable. Before magnetic navigation, long-distance ocean voyages were essentially impossible. Sailors could hug coastlines, island-hop across short distances, or make brief forays into open water, but sustained oceanic exploration was a death sentence.

The compass changed everything. When Columbus set sail in 1492, he carried compasses that descended directly from those Chinese lodestone spoons. His three ships - the Niña, Pinta, and Santa María - each carried multiple compasses, giving him the confidence to sail west into uncharted Atlantic waters for weeks without sight of land.

Columbus was trying to find a western route to Asia because the traditional eastern routes were controlled by Ottoman and Arab traders who charged enormous prices for spices, silk, and other luxury goods. He believed the Earth was much smaller than it actually was and thought he could reach Japan in just a few weeks of sailing west.

Instead, after 36 days at sea, he bumped into the Caribbean islands and spent the rest of his life convinced he had reached the outer islands of Asia. Columbus never realized he had found an entirely new continent. This geographic miscalculation accidentally opened up the Americas to European exploration and colonization, changing the course of world history.

When Vasco da Gama rounded the treacherous Cape of Good Hope in 1497, he relied on compass navigation to guide him through waters no European had ever mapped. Da Gama was breaking a trade monopoly that had lasted for centuries.

All the valuable goods from Asia - spices like pepper and cinnamon, silk, precious stones, and exotic medicines - had to travel overland through the Middle East before reaching Europe. This meant every European merchant had to buy these goods from Middle Eastern traders, who could charge whatever prices they wanted because they controlled the only route.

Da Gama's voyage around Africa to India created the first direct sea route from Europe to Asia, allowing Europeans to bypass the middlemen and trade directly with Asian producers. Magellan's attempt to circumnavigate the globe in 1519 was only conceivable because magnetic compasses allowed him to maintain course across the vast Pacific Ocean. Though Magellan died during the voyage, his expedition proved the Earth was round and much larger than anyone had imagined.

The compass made these voyages possible by solving navigation's fundamental problem: how to maintain direction when you can't see familiar landmarks, stars, or coastlines.

European Superstitions

Early European sailors often viewed compasses with suspicion bordering on superstition. A needle that always pointed north without any visible mechanism seemed like witchcraft to men accustomed to celestial navigation. Some refused to use compasses, convinced they were tools of the devil. Others worried about the legendary "lodestone mountains" that supposedly could pull all the iron nails from a ship's hull, leaving it to sink in splinters.

These fears gradually gave way to trust as the compass proved its reliability voyage after voyage. By the late 15th century, most European ships carried compasses as standard equipment. Columbus documented magnetic declination during his Atlantic crossing, noting that the needle didn't point exactly north but shifted slightly as he sailed west. His crew saw this shift and feared the laws of physics were breaking down. To prevent mutiny, Columbus allegedly recalibrated the compasses secretly, adjusting the cards underneath to make them appear to point true north.

Some sailors believed cursing while looking at a compass would offend its "magic" and lead them astray. They treated the compass as a moral guide that only worked for righteous people. Traditionalists who relied on stars and dead reckoning saw compass use as angering God and the spirits of the sea.

The compass remained the primary navigation tool for ships until the 20th century, when radio beacons and GPS began to supersede magnetic navigation. Even now, every ship carries magnetic compasses as backup systems, and compass apps in smartphones use the same basic principle that guided Chinese junks across the South China Sea a thousand years ago.

What began as a fortune-teller's prop became the key that unlocked the world's oceans, enabling global trade, cultural exchange, and the interconnected world we inhabit today. When you check directions on your phone or watch a ship navigate the harbor, you're witnessing the same magnetic principles that once seemed like magic to Chinese emperors. Can a simple piece of magnetized metal really trace a direct line from ancient superstition to modern globalization? The compass proves that sometimes the most revolutionary technologies start as the humblest curiosities.

Did You Know?

The Titanic had three magnetic compasses and a gyrocompass, but the ship's massive steel hull created such magnetic interference that compass readings could be off by several degrees. Like the Chinese fortune-tellers who first used lodestones, the crew thought they had reliable navigation tools, until physics reminded them that even revolutionary technology has its limits.

Mad Dog of the Middle East, The Eccentric Reign of Gaddafi

September 23, 2009. The United Nations General Assembly watches in stunned silence as Libya's Muammar Gaddafi takes the podium wearing flowing brown robes and an Africa-shaped brooch the size of a dinner plate. What follows is a 96-minute ramble that tears through diplomatic protocol like a sandstorm through silk curtains. He literally rips up the UN Charter, calls for the Security Council to be abolished, suggests swine flu was a laboratory weapon, and demands $7.7 trillion in reparations from former colonial powers. By the time he's finished, half the assembly has walked out and the other half is checking their watches, wondering if they're witnessing performance art or a mental breakdown.

Gaddafi was mental. No getting around it, no "misunderstood by the West," just sheer madness wrapped in revolutionary rhetoric and accessorized with an oil fortune. For 42 years, he ruled Libya like his personal theater of the absurd, mixing genuine anti-colonial sentiment with spectacular brutality, oil-funded

Pan-African dreams with state-sponsored terrorism. He was Che Guevara with a trust fund and serious boundary issues.

Revolutionary's Dawn

A 27-year-old army captain who looked like a cross between Omar Sharif and every mother's idea of a nice young man. On September 1, 1969, Gaddafi and his Free Officers Movement pulled off one of history's most polite coups. No shots fired, no blood spilled. They simply walked into Radio Benghazi, announced the monarchy was over, and asked King Idris (who was conveniently in Turkey for medical treatment) not to bother coming home.

The young Gaddafi had actual revolutionary credentials. Born to Bedouin parents in a tent near Sirte, he'd grown up listening to Radio Cairo's Gamal Abdel Nasser preach Arab nationalism while British and American bases dotted his homeland like colonial acne. At military academy, he secretly organized cells, read Nasser's *Philosophy of the Revolution*, and dreamed of an Arab renaissance that would stretch from the Atlantic to the Gulf.

His early moves suggested substance behind the swagger. He expelled British and American military bases, nationalized foreign oil companies, and kicked out Libya's 20,000-strong Italian community (some of whose families had been there for generations). Oil revenues, previously split between foreign companies and a compliant monarchy, now flowed directly into state coffers. Libya's per capita income jumped from $50 to over $8,000 in a decade.

Revolution, Gaddafi discovered, was the easy part. Governing required more than righteous anger and theatrical flair.

The Green Book and Other Delusions

In 1975, Gaddafi published his masterwork: *The Green Book*, subtitled "The Solution to the Problem of Democracy." If Mao had the Little Red Book, Gaddafi reasoned, why shouldn't Libya have its own ideological manual? The result reads like a political science textbook written by someone who'd never taken a political science class.

Gaddafi's "Third Universal Theory" rejected both capitalism and communism in favor of something he called "Jamahiriya" (state of the masses). In practice, this meant abolishing private property, banning political parties, and replacing government with a bewildering network of "People's Committees" that somehow made every citizen both ruler and ruled.

The theory was bonkers because it solved every problem by declaring it didn't exist. No unemployment if everyone works for themselves. No poverty if people only take what they need. No crime if society stops creating criminals. No conflict if everyone participates in "direct democracy" through committees that had no actual power because real decisions were made by the Brother Leader who officially didn't exist. Libya became a country where the constitution banned private property while Gaddafi lived in palaces, where "people's power" meant doing what Muammar suggested, and where direct democracy required a dictator to explain what the people really wanted.

Gaddafi wasn't just reshaping Libya's economy; he was redesigning reality itself. He moved the country to its own calendar (starting from the Prophet Muhammad's death rather than his birth), renamed months after his son and daughter, and declared that Libya had achieved "direct democracy" while simultaneously ruling it as a one-man show. When asked about this contradiction, he'd insist he held no official position, he was simply the "Brother Leader," offering guidance from the sidelines.

Terror's Patron Saint

By the late 1970s, Gaddafi's revolution had found its international voice, and that voice was screaming for blood. If Western powers had humiliated the Arab world through colonialism and support for Israel, then Western civilians were fair game for revenge. Libya became the Walmart of international terrorism, one-stop shopping for weapons, training, and funding with the customer service of a Swiss bank and the morality of a arms dealer.

The customer list read like a greatest hits of global mayhem. The IRA wanted Britain out of Northern Ireland and had no qualms about bombing pubs to make their point. The Red Army Faction was Germany's answer to 1960s radicalism gone homicidal, kidnapping industrialists and assassinating prosecutors in the name of anti-capitalist revolution. The Japanese Red Army took revolutionary tourism to new heights, hijacking planes to North Korea and machine-gunning passengers at Tel Aviv airport because international solidarity apparently required slaughtering random travelers. The Popular Front for the Liberation of Palestine pioneered airplane hijacking as political theater, turning commercial aviation into a battlefield for Palestinian nationalism. Abu Nidal's organization was Palestinian nationalism without the politics, pure sectarian murder that killed more Palestinians than Israelis and made everyone else look moderate by comparison.

Oil money that should have built schools and hospitals instead bought Kalashnikovs and Semtex. Libya was pumping 3 million barrels a day by the late 1970s, generating billions in revenue that Gaddafi diverted from development into his personal terrorism export business. If you had a grievance against the West and weren't too picky about methods, Tripoli would write you a check. Gaddafi's agents smuggled weapons in diplomatic pouches, ran training camps in the Libyan desert, and coordinated attacks across three continents.

The catalog of carnage was encyclopedic. After Palestinian terrorists killed Israeli athletes at the 1972 Munich Olympics, Gaddafi flew their bodies to Tripoli for a state funeral, complete with military honors and burial in a martyr's cemetery that became a pilgrimage site. He armed the IRA with thousands of tons of weapons, turning "The Troubles" into a decades-long nightmare powered by Libyan Semtex. UTA Flight 772 exploded over Niger in 1989, killing 170 people because Gaddafi was annoyed with French involvement in Chad. Abu Nidal's thugs hijacked Pan Am Flight 73 in Karachi, turning the cabin into a shooting gallery that left 20 dead. His hit squads stalked Libyan dissidents across European capitals, proving that Gaddafi's idea of diplomacy involved car bombs and silencers.

The West's response to this carnival of violence was breathtakingly feeble. When Palestinian terrorists massacred Israeli athletes at the 1972 Munich Olympics, the world watched in horror. When Gaddafi flew their corpses to Tripoli for a state funeral with full military honors, the world watched in embarrassed silence. Western governments that had condemned the attack somehow found themselves powerless to prevent a head of state from celebrating the killers as martyrs. Diplomatic immunity meant Libyan embassies became weapons depots. Oil revenues meant economic sanctions would hurt Western consumers more than Gaddafi. Cold War calculations meant nobody wanted to push Libya into Soviet arms. The result was a bizarre international system where everyone knew Libya was exporting terrorism, everyone condemned it in speeches, and everyone kept buying Libyan oil while Gaddafi's hit squads roamed their capitals.

The bill came due on April 5, 1986, when a bomb exploded at the La Belle discotheque in West Berlin, killing three people (including two American servicemen) and wounding 229. U.S. intelligence intercepted communications linking the attack directly to the Libyan embassy in East Berlin. Ten days later, 18 American F-111s took off from British bases and delivered 60 tons of ordnance to Libya, targeting Gaddafi's compound in Bab al-Azizia.

That attack was actually the second time in two years that Gaddafi had tested Western resolve with embassy terrorism. In 1984, a gunman in the Libyan embassy on London's St. James's Square shot and killed WPC Yvonne Fletcher, a police officer monitoring a peaceful anti-Gaddafi protest. The killer fired from an upper window, murdered a British police officer on British soil, then hid behind diplomatic immunity like a playground bully ducking behind his mother's skirts. The British surrounded the embassy for 11 days but couldn't legally storm it under international law. All 30 Libyan diplomats, including the killer, were eventually escorted to Heathrow and flown home to Tripoli. The murder weapon, a Sterling submachine gun, reportedly traveled with them in a diplomatic bag that British customs couldn't legally search. Gaddafi had discovered that embassies made perfect criminal hideouts.

Gaddafi survived the 1986 bombing (he was reportedly hiding in his bunker), and the message was clear enough. For most leaders, this might have prompted reflection. For Gaddafi, it was merely intermission.

Lockerbie's Shadow

Two years later, Pan Am Flight 103 exploded over Lockerbie, Scotland, killing 270 people. The investigation would eventually trace the bombing to Libyan agents, but at the time, the attack seemed like the inevitable escalation of Gaddafi's war on Western aviation. Libya had already been linked to attacks on airports in Rome and Vienna. Gaddafi had openly called for attacks on American interests worldwide. In the twisted logic of state-sponsored terrorism, civilian airliners had become legitimate military targets.

The Lockerbie bombing crossed a line that even Gaddafi's previous atrocities hadn't approached. This wasn't a military target or a nightclub frequented by soldiers; this was a passenger plane full of students, families, and Christmas travelers. Among the victims were 35 Syracuse University students returning from study abroad, their young lives snuffed out at 31,000 feet because a Libyan dictator had decided civilian aviation was a legitimate battlefield. The randomness was the point. Terror works best when nobody feels safe anywhere.

The investigation became one of history's most complex criminal inquiries, a four-year hunt that eventually turned on a fragment of circuit board smaller than a fingernail. This tiny piece of evidence, recovered from the Scottish countryside, was traced to a timer used exclusively by Libyan intelligence. The painstaking detective work led to the indictment of two Libyan agents, Abdelbaset al-Megrahi and Lamin Khalifah Fhimah, in 1991. Gaddafi refused to hand them over for nearly a decade, turning international justice into a diplomatic chess game where the families of 270 victims were pawns.

The compromise trial in 2001 at a former U.S. airbase in the Netherlands found al-Megrahi guilty on 270 counts of murder. Eight years later, Scotland released

73

him on compassionate grounds due to terminal cancer. Gaddafi welcomed the convicted bomber home with a hero's reception, crowds cheering as al-Megrahi stepped off the plane in Tripoli. Even when caught red-handed, even when forced to pay compensation, even when one of his agents was convicted of mass murder, Gaddafi couldn't resist one final insult to the victims' families.

The pattern was clear. From the gunman who killed WPC Fletcher walking free from Heathrow to the Lockerbie bomber receiving a hero's welcome in Tripoli, Gaddafi had discovered that Western legal systems were designed for civilized opponents who played by gentleman's rules, not for dictators who treated international law like a 24-hour convenience store they could rob whenever they needed something.

Diplomatic immunity was meant to protect embassies from host governments, not to shield murderers. Compassionate release was designed for remorseful criminals facing death, not for unrepentant terrorists whose governments would throw them parades. Extradition treaties assumed both parties wanted justice, not that one side would use legal proceedings as performance art.

Gaddafi gamed every system because he understood something Western democracies couldn't quite grasp: when one player follows the rules and the other treats them as suggestions, the rule-follower loses every time.

International sanctions followed, turning Libya into a pariah state, a diplomatic untouchable shunned by the global community like a plague carrier at a dinner party. Airlines couldn't fly there, banks couldn't do business there, diplomats couldn't visit there. Libya was cut off from the international financial system, banned from purchasing aircraft parts, and excluded from sporting events. The UN even froze Libyan assets abroad and imposed an arms embargo. The same theatrical instincts that made him celebrate dead terrorists would soon transform him into one of history's most flamboyant dictators.

Theater of the Absurd

Isolation had freed Gaddafi from any pretense of normal behavior. Without Western approval to lose, he could indulge every megalomaniacal whim, every eccentric obsession, every bizarre impulse that crossed his mind. The result was a 20-year performance art piece staged by a man with unlimited oil money and serious boundary issues.

The Amazonian Guard, his all-female bodyguard unit, became his signature accessory. Handpicked for loyalty and lethality, these women underwent rigorous training in martial arts, weapons handling, and, presumably, the fine art of looking intimidating while wearing high heels and military fatigues. They were required to be virgins and take vows of chastity, a twisted purity test that made them seem more like warrior nuns than security personnel. Western journalists couldn't get enough of them, which was exactly the point. While they obsessed over the gender politics of his security detail, Gaddafi was quietly rebuilding his international networks.

His diplomatic style became equally theatrical. He'd arrive at summits in Bedouin tents that his advance team would pitch on the host country's soil, complete with camels, carpets, and a full desert camp aesthetic. The boy who'd grown up in a goat-hair tent moving with his family's herds now forced world leaders to visit him in designer versions of his childhood home.

At the 2009 G8 summit in Italy, his team initially tried to pitch the tent on a polo field in Rome before settling for a historic public park, forcing the Italian government to shut down significant portions to accommodate one man's camping fantasy. New York rejected his attempts to set up in Central Park, and New Jersey suburbs turned him away after public outcry. The tent wasn't just a gimmick; it was a statement about authenticity, simplicity, and his connection to Libya's pre-colonial roots. That it also allowed him to control every aspect of his environment, from temperature to acoustics to who got invited inside, was a happy bonus.

The costumes evolved with each occasion. Military uniforms gave way to flowing robes, which gave way to increasingly outlandish combinations of traditional and modern dress. At the 2009 G8 summit in Italy, he showed up wearing a military uniform decorated with a large photograph of Omar Mukhtar, the Libyan resistance leader hanged by Mussolini in 1931. The message was subtle as a brick through a window.

Obsessions and Fixations

His gift-giving was equally bizarre. Instead of standard diplomatic trinkets, he presented world leaders with custom gold watches featuring his own face and lockets containing his photograph. These weren't gifts; they were personal artifacts meant to assert his eccentric personality on the world stage, final absurd flourishes to diplomatic encounters that had already descended into farce.

No relationship better captured this psychological complexity than his documented obsession with Condoleezza Rice. By the mid-2000s, Libya had grudgingly compensated Lockerbie victims and abandoned its nuclear weapons program, earning a cautious Western rehabilitation. When the former U.S. Secretary of State visited Tripoli in 2008 as part of this diplomatic thaw, Gaddafi presented her with a DVD of photos set to a song called "Black Flower in the White House." His compound contained a private room devoted entirely to Rice memorabilia, photos, news clippings, and videos arranged like a teenager's bedroom shrine.

"I support my darling black African woman," he told Al-Jazeera. "I admire and am very proud of the way she leans back and gives orders to the Arab leaders." The comment managed to be simultaneously creepy, patronizing, and politically tone-deaf. Peak Gaddafi in three sentences.

His phobias were as intense as his fixations. Despite ruling a country larger than Alaska, Gaddafi was terrified of flying, preferring to travel by armored Mercedes convoy even for international trips. His fear of assassination led him to employ multiple body doubles, sleep in a different location each night, and surround himself with an ever-expanding security apparatus that eventually employed an estimated 10% of Libya's adult population.

The domestic surveillance network he built would have impressed the Stasi. Every neighborhood had its informants, every institution its watchers. University professors knew their lectures were monitored; students learned to whisper dissent or keep it to themselves entirely. The mukhabarat (secret police) had files on virtually every Libyan citizen, creating a society where trust became a luxury few could afford.

Pan-African Dreams

As the new millennium dawned, Gaddafi reinvented himself once again, this time as Africa's self-appointed unifier. Having been rejected by the Arab world (his fellow Arab leaders found him embarrassing) and isolated by the West, he turned south with the fervor of a convert.

The African Union became his pet project, funded largely by Libyan oil money. In 2008, a gathering of traditional African rulers bestowed upon him the title "King of Kings," a ceremony he embraced with characteristic lack of irony. His new wardrobe reflected this pivot: flowing robes decorated with maps of Africa, jewelry shaped like the continent, and headwear that seemed designed to make him look like a cross between Nelson Mandela and a Vegas showman.

Gaddafi's vision of African unity was as much about ego as ideology. His proposed "United States of Africa" would, naturally, have him as its first president. He funded liberation movements, bankrolled infrastructure projects, and offered Libyan passports to African migrants, not out of Pan-African solidarity, but because he saw Africa as his natural sphere of influence, a continent-sized stage for his ambitions.

Many Africans wanted nothing to do with him. His intervention in Chad's civil war had been a disaster. His meddling in Sudan's internal affairs annoyed Khartoum. His grandiose pronouncements about African unity sounded suspiciously like the colonial paternalism he claimed to oppose.

The Reckoning

By 2011, the contradictions that had always defined Gaddafi's rule finally caught up with him. The Arab Spring, a wave of popular uprisings that had already toppled dictators in Tunisia and Egypt, reached Libya in February, starting with protests in Benghazi that quickly spread across the country. Libyans who had endured 42 years of his theatrical tyranny finally said enough.

Gaddafi's response was characteristically unhinged. He blamed the uprising on foreign agents, al-Qaeda, and drug-addled youth high on hallucinogenic pills allegedly distributed by rebels. In a rambling speech, he vowed to hunt down protesters "house by house, room by room" and cleanse Libya of "rats and cockroaches." The man who had once promised to bring dignity to the Arab world was now threatening to massacre his own people.

The international response was swift and devastating. NATO airstrikes destroyed Libya's air defenses, grounded its air force, and systematically dismantled the military infrastructure that had kept Gaddafi in power for four decades. Within months, rebel forces were advancing on Tripoli while Gaddafi's regime crumbled around him.

His end came on October 20, 2011, in a drainage culvert outside Sirte, the city of his birth. The boy who'd grown up in a goat-hair tent in the same desert scrubland now cowered in a concrete pipe, blood streaming from his head. Captured by rebels, he was beaten, sodomized with a bayonet, and shot to death. Cell phone videos of his final moments spread across the internet, providing a grotesque coda to a life lived in pursuit of historical significance. His body was displayed in a commercial freezer in Misrata while Libyans queued up to take selfies with their former dictator. The man who had once declared "I am Libya, Libya is me" had become a tourist attraction.

The Libya he left behind was a shattered collection of tribes with a flag, just as it had been when he seized power 42 years earlier. Those Italian colonial administrators who had cobbled together three Ottoman provinces into a country would have recognized the chaos: competing governments in Tripoli and Benghazi, tribal militias controlling oil fields, and borders that existed only on maps while smugglers and migrants moved freely across the Sahara.

The revolution he had promised in 1969 had finally arrived, but it looked nothing like the utopia he'd sketched in his Green Book. The same oil wealth that funded his terrorism export business now fueled militia warfare. The Bedouin tents were gone, replaced by pickup trucks mounted with anti-aircraft guns.

Libya in 2025 remains what it always was: a geographic expression searching for a nation to inhabit it. The lines drawn by European bureaucrats in distant capitals still can't contain the forces that Gaddafi spent 42 years trying to harness but never understood. Muammar Gaddafi, the man who spent a lifetime trying to write himself into history as a revolutionary hero, ended up proving that some performances are too ridiculous to survive contact with reality. His Condoleezza Rice scrapbook probably survived him.

Did You Know?

Gaddafi once tried to pitch his tent in Donald Trump's backyard in Bedford, New York, during a 2009 UN visit. Trump took the money, then had local authorities shut it down. Even the future president had limits.

Libya's flag under Gaddafi was just solid green, the only national flag in history with no design, insignia, or other colors. It perfectly captured his approach to governance: why complicate things when you can just paint everything one color and call it revolutionary?

Gaddafi's female bodyguards were required to take an oath of virginity, but several later revealed they were repeatedly raped by the leader they were protecting. The "revolutionary feminist" was just another predator with better PR.

His son Saif al-Islam owned a pet tiger that once escaped in central Tripoli, mauling a gardener before being recaptured. When your family pet mauls the help, you might be a dictator.

Iron Swords and Ivory Gallows, Cromwell in Ireland

September 11, 1649. The walls of Drogheda crumble under English cannon fire as Oliver Cromwell watches from horseback, Bible tucked beneath his breastplate, sword gleaming in the autumn light. Smoke and screams fill the air as his New Model Army pours through the breach like water through a dam. What follows will be remembered in Ireland for centuries, not as liberation, but as the day righteousness revealed its true face.

"No quarter," Cromwell orders. Take no prisoners. Spare no one who bore arms against Parliament. The soldiers who had sung psalms before battle now club priests to death in their churches and hunt civilians through narrow streets. By evening, 2,800 defenders and townsfolk lie dead. Cromwell will write to Parliament that this was "the righteous judgment of God upon these barbarous wretches," as if the Almighty personally approved of splitting skulls with musket butts.

Cromwell in Ireland was part crusading saint, part genocidal conqueror, wholly convinced that God was on his side. For four years, he and his successors would remake Ireland through sword and famine, turning conquest into a holy mission and ethnic cleansing into divine justice. The man who had executed a king for tyranny was about to show Ireland what real tyranny looked like.

The Righteous Invader

Cromwell crossed the Irish Sea in August 1649 with 12,000 battle-hardened veterans and a head full of biblical certainty. England had just emerged from a civil war that killed a king and established a republic. Ireland, which had rebelled in 1641 and remained partially controlled by Catholic Confederates and Royalist holdouts, represented unfinished business in the Puritan project of remaking the British Isles.

The 1641 Irish Rebellion had indeed involved massacres of Protestant settlers, perhaps 4,000 dead, though English propaganda inflated the numbers to 200,000 or more, a figure that would have required the Protestants to outnumber the Irish tenfold in some counties, remarkable demographic engineering for the 17th century. Cromwell genuinely believed he was avenging those deaths, carrying out delayed justice for what he saw as Catholic barbarism. That the vast majority of Ireland's population had nothing to do with those killings was irrelevant. In Cromwell's worldview, Catholic Ireland was collectively guilty, a nest of papist vipers that needed cleansing.

His army was perfectly suited to the task. The New Model Army had spent eight years learning how to kill efficiently while maintaining the fiction that they were doing God's work. These weren't medieval knights bound by chivalric codes; they were professional soldiers who could justify any atrocity with a psalm. For these men, every victory wasn't just tactical success but proof of divine favor. Puritan theology taught that the elect could recognize God's will through the results of their actions. Losing a battle meant their faith needed testing; winning confirmed their righteousness. This doctrine made violence not just permissible but a moral imperative. When you believed that military success proved God's approval, slaughtering Irish Catholics became evidence of your own salvation.

Ireland in 1649 was a patchwork of competing authorities. The Confederate Catholics controlled much of the south and west, Royalist Protestants held scattered strongholds, and English Parliamentary forces occupied Dublin and a few coastal towns. The island was already exhausted by eight years of intermittent warfare, its economy shattered, its people surviving on hope and stubbornness. Cromwell was about to test the limits of both.

A Lesson in Terror

Drogheda was chosen for shock value. The medieval port town, thirty miles north of Dublin, controlled the main road between English strongholds. Its walls were strong, its garrison determined, and its symbolic value enormous. If Cromwell could take Drogheda brutally enough, other towns might surrender without a fight. Terror, he understood, was more efficient than siege warfare.

The assault began on September 10 with a bombardment that reduced sections of the medieval wall to rubble. When the first infantry assault failed, Cromwell ordered the famous "no quarter" that would echo through Irish history. According to the laws of war, a garrison that refused to surrender after a practicable breach could be put to the sword. Cromwell was technically within his rights. He was also about to exceed those rights so thoroughly that even his own soldiers would be sickened.

The slaughter lasted hours. English soldiers bayoneted wounded defenders, hunted civilians through cellars and attics, and burned alive anyone who sought sanctuary in churches. One group of defenders retreated to the church tower of St. Peter's; Cromwell's men piled pews against the door and set them ablaze, roasting the garrison alive. When Catholic priests were found, they were beaten to death with clubs, their blood literally staining the church floors.

Cromwell's own account to Parliament was chillingly matter-of-fact. "I am persuaded that this is a righteous judgment of God upon these barbarous wretches, who have imbrued their hands in so much innocent blood," he wrote, as if the Almighty personally approved of splitting skulls with musket butts and had simply forgotten to send a memo about it earlier. He was particularly pleased that several Catholic priests had been killed, writing that "their friars were knocked on the head promiscuously." The man who claimed to serve the Prince of Peace had just overseen a massacre.

The slaughter was immediate and profound. Word of Drogheda's fate spread across Ireland faster than Cromwell's army could march. Towns that might have resisted began discussing surrender. The Irish poet witnessed "women with their hair about their ears" fleeing westward with tales of English savagery. Cromwell had achieved his strategic objective: terror had become his most effective weapon.

Wexford: When "Accidents" Happen

A month later at Wexford, Cromwell proved that Drogheda was no aberration. The coastal town in the southeast corner of Ireland was another Royalist stronghold, another example to be made. What happened there would cement Cromwell's reputation as either a master strategist or a war criminal, depending on which side of the Irish Sea you asked.

The siege of Wexford began with the usual formalities. Cromwell demanded surrender, the garrison refused, negotiations dragged on. But while talks continued, something went wrong. English soldiers breached the town walls while surrender terms were still being discussed. What followed was either a tragic breakdown in military discipline or a conveniently timed "accident" that allowed Cromwell to claim plausible deniability.

The results were identical to Drogheda, wholesale slaughter. Some 2,000 defenders and civilians died in the streets of Wexford. Churches again became charnel houses. The harbor filled with bodies as people tried to escape by sea only to drown under the weight of armor and panic. Cromwell expressed regret about the timing but not the outcome, writing that "it hath not without cause been deeply set upon our hearts, that we intending better to this place than so great a ruin, hoping the town might be of more use to you and your army, yet God would not have it so."

God, it seemed, had a remarkable talent for ensuring that Irish towns were destroyed just when Cromwell needed examples made. Similar patterns would repeat across Ireland, negotiations would collapse at convenient moments, military discipline would mysteriously fail, and Irish blood would flow while English commanders expressed pious regret about divine will overruling their merciful intentions. Cromwell had discovered that righteousness was the perfect shield for ruthlessness, especially when God himself was willing to serve as your alibi.

The "accidents" at Wexford established a template that Cromwell's subordinates would follow long after he returned to England. When you could blame God for military atrocities, accountability became a theological rather than legal question. Cromwell had discovered that righteousness was the perfect shield for ruthlessness.

Famine by Design

After the shock victories of 1649, the conquest settled into a grinding campaign of starvation. The great sieges were finished; now came the harder work of breaking Irish resistance through hunger. Cromwell and his successor Henry Ireton understood that Ireland's scattered guerrilla bands could be defeated not through battle but through systematic destruction of the food supply.

The policy was elegantly simple: if you couldn't catch Irish fighters, you could starve them. English forces burned crops still standing in fields, slaughtered livestock, destroyed grain stores, and poisoned wells. The aim was to create conditions where continued resistance became impossible, where Irish families would choose English rule over watching their children starve.

The results exceeded even Cromwell's expectations. By 1650, artificial famine gripped much of Ireland. Travelers reported seeing corpses littering roadsides, entire villages abandoned, and survivors reduced to eating grass and bark. The destruction was so systematic that even fertile areas became wastelands. One English officer wrote that Ireland had become "a country of skulls," its population scattered to the winds.

Contemporary observers struggled to quantify the devastation. Population estimates suggest that between 15% and 40% of Ireland's people died during the Cromwellian conquest, whether from violence, starvation, or disease. The demographic collapse was so severe that some regions didn't recover their pre-1649 population levels for over a century. Cromwell had achieved something remarkable, genocide disguised as military strategy.

The famine wasn't an unfortunate side effect of war; it was war by other means. Cromwell's letters reveal a clear understanding that hunger would accomplish what sieges couldn't: the complete submission of Catholic Ireland. He was systematically destroying not just Irish resistance but Irish civilization itself, creating conditions so desperate that survival would require collaboration with English rule.

Irish folk memory preserved the horror in ways that official histories couldn't capture. Stories emerged of mothers eating their dead children, of priests blessing grass before families consumed it, of entire communities simply disappearing. These weren't military casualties; they were the price of Cromwell's vision of a godly Ireland purged of Catholic "barbarism."

To Hell or Connaught

By 1653, organized Irish resistance had collapsed, but Cromwell's work was far from finished. Military conquest was only the first phase; now came the social revolution that would remake Irish society from the ground up. The policy that emerged would be summarized in five words that still echo through Irish history: "To Hell or to Connaught."

The Act of Settlement of 1652 was ethnic cleansing with legal paperwork. Catholic landowners, who had controlled roughly 70% of Irish land before the rebellion, were given a choice, relocate west of the River Shannon to the barren province of Connaught, or face execution. The policy, in its elegant simplicity, gave the Irish the option of either starving slowly in a desolate landscape or dying quickly. A generous offer, if you considered the alternative. The most fertile lands in Ireland would be redistributed to English Protestant settlers, soldiers who had served in the conquest, and "Adventurers" who had financed the campaign. These Adventurers were not soldiers but financiers, wealthy London merchants and gentry who had invested in the conquest with promises of Irish land in return.

They saw Ireland not as a battlefield for God but as a vast real estate opportunity. Their financial stake in the war ensured that Parliament's policies were driven not just by piety but by profit, creating a powerful lobby for the harshest possible measures against the Catholic population. The conquest had to succeed completely because too much money depended on it.

The transplantation was brutal in its scope and efficiency. The logistical precision was as cruel as its goal. Parliamentary commissioners, armed with maps and legal decrees, systematically marked out Catholic landholdings. Families were given deadlines, often just weeks, to sell their crops and livestock at fire-sale prices and begin the long march west. The roads became rivers of human suffering, with the elderly and sick often dying along the way, their bodies left unburied as testament to the new order. One observer described roads clogged with refugees, "old men, women great with child, and children" all heading toward a province that even in good times could barely feed its existing inhabitants.

The mathematical precision of the land grab revealed the systematic nature of Cromwell's vision. Protestant ownership of Irish land jumped from roughly

30% to 80% in a few years. Catholic landownership, meanwhile, fell to about 10% of the total, concentrated in the poorest western counties. This wasn't military occupation; it was demographic replacement on a continental scale.

The human cost extended beyond property seizure. An estimated 50,000-100,000 Irish were transported to English colonies in the Caribbean and North America, many as indentured servants barely distinguishable from slaves. Irish children were particular targets for transportation, seen as more suitable for "civilization" in Protestant colonies. Families were systematically broken apart, their children shipped to Barbados while parents died in Connaught bogs.

Cromwell's supporters defended the policy as both practical and moral. Practical because it solved the problem of Irish rebellion by removing the population capable of sustaining it. Moral because it offered Catholic Irish the chance at redemption through exile and hard labor in godly colonies. The logic was impeccable if you accepted the premise that Catholic Ireland was collectively guilty and Protestant England collectively innocent.

The Righteous Aftermath

The Ireland that emerged from Cromwell's conquest was unrecognizable. The old Gaelic social order had been obliterated, replaced by a Protestant settler society that governed a dispossessed Catholic majority. The transformation was so complete that visitors from continental Europe struggled to understand how such systematic change had been accomplished in so short a time.

Dublin became the capital of a colonial society as rigidly stratified as any in the Americas. English Protestant landlords controlled vast estates worked by Irish Catholic tenants who had no legal rights, no political representation, and no prospect of recovering their lost status. The Penal Laws that would follow in subsequent decades merely codified arrangements that Cromwell's conquest had established through violence.

The demographic impact was staggering and permanent. Entire regions had been depopulated and repopulated. English Protestant settlements dotted landscapes that had been Catholic for over a millennium. Irish Gaelic, which had been the majority language before 1649, retreated to western peninsulas and mountain valleys. The cultural genocide was as thorough as the physical conquest.

Cromwell's own assessment of his Irish campaign was characteristically self-congratulatory. Writing to Parliament, he claimed that Ireland was now "a clean paper" upon which godly government could write a new history. The metaphor was revealing, Cromwell saw the Irish people not as fellow Christians to be converted but as ink to be erased so that better text could take its place, never mind the bloodstains and scorched marks left behind on the "paper" itself.

The English view of the conquest emphasized its necessity and divine approval. Cromwell had solved the Irish problem that had vexed English governments for centuries. He had secured Protestant England's western flank, created a profitable colony, and demonstrated that republican virtue could achieve what royal incompetence had failed to accomplish. The methods were perhaps harsh, but God had clearly blessed the results.

Irish collective memory told a different story. Cromwell became a name to frighten children, a byword for Protestant cruelty, a figure so associated with suffering that "the curse of Cromwell" remained a common oath centuries later. Folk tales emerged of supernatural intervention on Cromwell's behalf, as if normal human evil couldn't explain the thoroughness of the conquest.

The Saint and the Butcher

The paradox of Cromwell in Ireland is that both his admirers and his enemies were right about him. He was genuinely motivated by religious conviction, sincerely believed he was doing God's work, and created institutions that would govern Ireland for centuries. He was also responsible for one of the most systematic campaigns of ethnic cleansing in early modern European history.

The contradiction wasn't accidental; it was essential to Cromwell's worldview. Puritan theology taught that the elect could recognize God's will through the success of their enterprises. Military victory proved divine approval; demographic collapse among enemies confirmed their wickedness. The more thoroughly Cromwell destroyed Catholic Ireland, the more convinced he became of his own righteousness.

This theological certainty made Cromwell more dangerous than conventional tyrants. A secular conqueror might be satisfied with political submission and economic exploitation. A religious conqueror needed spiritual transformation, which meant eliminating not just resistance but the culture that sustained it. Cromwell wasn't content to rule Ireland; he wanted to recreate it in England's Protestant image.

The efficiency of the Cromwellian conquest reflected the intersection of religious zeal and military innovation. The New Model Army was perhaps history's first ideologically motivated professional military force, capable of sustaining campaigns that would have broken purely mercenary forces. When soldiers believed they were fighting for eternal salvation, tactical setbacks became tests of faith rather than reasons for retreat.

Modern Ireland still bears the scars of decisions made in Westminster during the 1650s. The Protestant Ascendancy that would dominate Irish politics until the twentieth century traced its origins to Cromwellian land grants. The sectarian divisions that would define Ulster for centuries were hardened by transplantations that separated Catholic and Protestant populations into distinct geographical areas.

Even the language of modern Irish politics echoes Cromwellian themes. The partition of Ireland in 1921 followed lines that Cromwell would have recognized, dividing the island between Protestant areas that remained loyal to England and Catholic regions that sought independence. The "plantation" model that Cromwell perfected in Ireland would later be applied in Scotland and North America, creating patterns of settlement and resistance that shaped English colonial policy for centuries.

Judgment Day

The Ireland that Cromwell left behind in 1650 resembled a vast crime scene more than a conquered province. Population estimates suggest that the island had lost between one-fifth and two-fifths of its inhabitants in four years. The survivors inhabited a landscape dotted with ruined towns, abandoned villages, and mass graves that would be discovered centuries later.

Yet Cromwell's reputation in England remained largely intact. He had solved the Irish problem, secured valuable lands for Protestant settlement, and demonstrated that godly government could accomplish through righteousness what corrupt monarchies had failed to achieve through compromise. The Irish campaign was seen not as an aberration but as proof that divine providence favored the English republic.

The Protestant Ascendancy that emerged from Cromwell's conquest wasn't a natural development but deliberate social engineering. For generations, Irish Catholics remained systematically disenfranchised, excluded from politics, law, and landownership by policies rooted in Cromwellian notions that they were "unfit" to hold power. The sectarian geography he created, Protestant settlements overlooking Catholic tenancies, became the template for British colonial rule worldwide.

The legal frameworks developed to justify Irish land confiscation would be applied to later colonial enterprises from North America to Australia. The rhetorical strategies used to dehumanize Irish Catholics, portraying them as barbarous and unfit for civilization, would be recycled to justify violence against other non-Protestant populations. Cromwell had pioneered the art of genocide with paperwork.

Irish folk memory preserved aspects of the conquest that official histories ignored. Songs and stories passed down through generations captured details about community destruction, family separation, and cultural erasure that weren't recorded in English administrative documents. These oral traditions kept alive a version of events that contradicted English claims about necessary pacification and grateful liberation.

The theological dimensions of Cromwell's Irish campaign also had lasting implications. The conquest demonstrated that Protestant righteousness could justify almost any level of violence against Catholic populations. This precedent would influence English attitudes toward Catholic France, Spain, and other European powers for generations. Cromwell had proved that religious war could be both profitable and morally satisfying.

The ultimate contradiction of Cromwell's Irish campaign was its demonstration that republican virtue could be more tyrannical than royal corruption. The Commonwealth he established was more systematically oppressive than any previous English government had been. By claiming divine authority for political decisions, Cromwell made criticism tantamount to blasphemy and resistance equivalent to apostasy.

The partition of Ireland in 1921, dividing the island between the independent Irish Free State and Northern Ireland, followed lines that Cromwell would have recognized. The border largely separated Protestant unionist populations from Catholic nationalist ones, perpetuating sectarian divisions hardened by 17th-century policies. The conflict known as "The Troubles," which consumed Northern Ireland from the 1960s through the 1990s, was fought over the same fundamental questions of land, identity, and political power that Cromwell had tried to settle with sword and statute.

Irish republicans fighting British soldiers in Belfast and Derry saw themselves continuing a struggle that began with Cromwell's New Model Army. Murals and songs from the era depicted him as the eternal symbol of British oppression. The very geography of the conflict, sectarian enclaves and peace walls, reflected social stratification and religious segregation that began in the 1650s.

Cromwell died in 1658, convinced that history would vindicate his Irish policies. In England, where his reputation remained largely positive until the twentieth century, that vindication seemed plausible. In Ireland, where his name became synonymous with Protestant supremacy and Catholic suffering, the judgment was less forgiving. The divided legacy reflects the divided nature of the man himself, a liberator who enslaved, a saint who slaughtered, a revolutionary who created the most systematic tyranny Ireland had ever experienced.

The curse of Cromwell lived on in Irish memory not because the Irish were incapable of forgiveness, but because forgiveness requires acknowledgment of wrongdoing. English histories of the conquest continued to emphasize its necessity and success long after its human costs became undeniable. Until England grappled honestly with what Cromwell had done in its name, Ireland would remember him not as a complex historical figure but as a symbol of everything that English rule had meant for the Irish people.

Even Brexit negotiations in the 21st century stumbled over the Northern Ireland border, a line that exists because Cromwell's demographic engineering created two incompatible visions of Irish identity. The man who claimed to have written Ireland's future on a "clean paper" instead authored a story that no one has yet figured out how to end.

Did You Know?

Modern Ireland's GDP statistics are so skewed by multinational tax arrangements that economists invented a new metric called "GNI*" just to measure the actual Irish economy. Cromwell conquered Ireland for land; Silicon Valley conquered it for tax loopholes.

The Irish language has no word for "yes" or "no" - responses are given by repeating the verb from the question. After centuries of English rule that began with Cromwell's conquest, maybe the Irish just got tired of giving direct answers to authority figures.

In the Dreamtime's Scales, The Rainbow Serpent

The Rainbow Serpent is perhaps Australia's most ancient and enduring creation story, told by Aboriginal peoples across the continent for thousands of years. This is living mythology that continues to shape how Indigenous Australians understand their relationship with the land, water, and natural law.

Deep in Arnhem Land, on rock faces that have weathered fifty thousand seasons, ancient hands painted a serpent whose colors still shimmer in the morning light. Ochre and charcoal trace the creature's massive coils across stone, each scale rendered with precision that speaks of deep reverence. The painting is at least six thousand years old, perhaps more. The ochres themselves came from the sacred earth, red from iron oxide, yellow from clay, white from pipe clay, connecting the art to the land in an unbroken circle of creation. Around a campfire in 1920, an Aboriginal elder named Namatjira points to these images and begins a story that his grandfather told him, and his grandfather's grandfather before that.

"In the beginning," he says, his voice carrying the weight of countless retellings, "the world was flat and empty. No mountains, no rivers, no life stirring above the ground. Everything that would be lay sleeping beneath the earth, waiting."

Then the Rainbow Serpent stirred….

The World-Shaper

Before there was time as we understand it, the world existed in the Dreamtime, a realm where creation and existence flowed together like water finding its course. The land stretched endlessly, featureless and silent, while beneath its surface, all potential life waited in darkness. The Rainbow Serpent emerged from this primordial earth not as destroyer but as awakener. Massive beyond comprehension, its scales caught light that didn't yet exist and threw it back as color itself.

As the great creature moved across the empty land, its body carved valleys and riverbeds in the earth. Where it paused to rest, permanent waterholes formed, springs that would flow for millennia. The serpent's wake became the rivers that would sustain life, its resting places the sacred pools that would never run dry even in the harshest drought. Where other creation stories speak of gods commanding from on high, the Aboriginal peoples tell of a serpent that shaped the world through movement, through the simple act of traveling from place to place.

The Rainbow Serpent possessed the power to wake the sleeping animals. In some tellings, it commanded the frogs, bloated with hoarded water, to release their stores and fill the newly carved channels. In others, it called forth each creature by name, teaching them their purpose and their place in the great web

97

of existence. The kangaroo learned to bound across open ground, the crocodile to guard the waterways, the birds to carry messages between earth and sky.

Most sacred of all, the serpent created the rainbow itself. When rain clouds gathered and the sun broke through, Aboriginal peoples would see the great creature traveling between waterholes, its presence bridging earth and sky in bands of luminous color. Each color carried meaning: red for the life-blood that flows through all living things, yellow for the sun's warming power, blue and green for the waters and vegetation that sustain existence, purple for the spirit world that touches the physical realm. The rainbow was not mere meteorology but the visible sign of the serpent's ongoing care for the world it had created.

Creation, in Aboriginal understanding, was not a single act but an ongoing responsibility. The Rainbow Serpent did not simply make the world and withdraw; it remained present, watching, ensuring that the laws governing the relationship between all living things were observed. This benevolent creator could become a terrible judge when those laws were broken.

The stories tell of groups who forgot their obligations to the land and to each other. Perhaps they polluted a sacred waterhole, or hunted in forbidden areas, or violated the complex kinship laws that governed Aboriginal society. When such transgressions occurred, the Rainbow Serpent's response was swift and catastrophic. In one story preserved by the Yolngu people of Arnhem Land, two sisters ignore warnings and approach a sacred site associated with Yurlunggur, their name for the Rainbow Serpent. Their presence at the forbidden place awakens the great creature's anger. It rises from the depths, swallowing the women and their camp before retreating again to the depths.

Later, remorseful, it regurgitates them, but they are transformed, reborn as initiated beings who understand the sacred laws they had violated.

Floods that sweep away settlements, droughts that last for years, storms that reshape the landscape itself, all might be attributed to the Rainbow Serpent's displeasure. But these punishments were not arbitrary acts of divine anger; they were corrections, painful lessons intended to restore the proper balance between human behavior and natural law. Those who violated sacred law might find themselves changed into landscape features, rocks, or animals, becoming permanent reminders of the consequences of forgetting one's proper relationship with the land. These laws were precise and complex, covering everything from respect for Elders and proper protocols for entering another group's territory, to taboos around speaking the names of the deceased. The Rainbow Serpent enforced not just environmental respect but the entire web of social relationships that kept Aboriginal communities in harmony with each other and their surroundings.

Many Names, Living Waters

Across the vast expanse of Aboriginal Australia, the Rainbow Serpent appears in hundreds of variations, each adapted to local geography and cultural needs. In Western Australia, it is known as Wagyl, said to have carved the Swan River and to rest beneath the hills of Perth. In the Northern Territory, the Yolngu speak of Yurlunggur, while other groups tell of Ngalyod, Ungud, or Goorialla. Despite the varied names and regional differences, certain elements remain constant: the serpent is always associated with water, with creation, and with the rainbow that appears after rain.

Some versions portray the serpent as male, others as female, still others as possessing both genders or transcending gender entirely. In desert regions, where water is particularly precious, the serpent is often depicted as female, a mother figure whose life-giving waters flow from her body. In coastal areas, where the serpent's influence extends to the sea, it might be portrayed as male, a powerful father whose movements create tides and currents. The story's adaptability speaks to its profound truth within Aboriginal culture, each community emphasizing aspects most relevant to their particular environment while maintaining connection to a shared understanding of the natural world's spiritual dimensions.

The Rainbow Serpent stories are not relics of a vanished past but living elements of contemporary Aboriginal culture. When storm clouds gather over the Australian landscape and rainbows arc between sky and earth, many Aboriginal people still see the great serpent traveling between its sacred places. Children learn the stories not as quaint folklore but as practical wisdom about reading weather patterns, respecting water sources, and understanding their responsibilities to the land.

Modern Aboriginal communities continue to regard certain waterholes as sacred sites associated with the Rainbow Serpent. These places are protected not only for their cultural significance but because the stories emphasize their crucial role in maintaining the ecological balance of surrounding areas. The serpent's mythological presence serves as a form of environmental protection that has preserved crucial water sources for thousands of years.

The Dreamtime stories are inseparable from the songlines that crisscross the continent, invisible highways of music and memory that trace the Rainbow Serpent's ancient journeys. These songs serve as mnemonic maps, each verse corresponding to a geographical feature created by the serpent's passage. Aboriginal travelers could navigate vast distances by following these musical pathways, the rhythm and melody encoding precise directions, water sources, and sacred sites. The songs themselves are considered living entities, requiring careful preservation and proper transmission from one generation to the next.

Eternal Coils

The Rainbow Serpent shares certain characteristics with serpent figures found in mythologies worldwide. Like the Mesopotamian Tiamat, the Norse Jormungandr, or the Hindu Shesha, the Aboriginal serpent represents primordial creative and destructive power. Water serpents appear in the mythologies of cultures as diverse as those of ancient Egypt, pre-Columbian Mexico, and traditional China, suggesting that the association between serpents, water, and creation may reflect fundamental human responses to natural phenomena.

Yet the Rainbow Serpent remains distinctly Aboriginal in its emphasis on ongoing presence rather than distant creation. Unlike many world serpents that represent chaos overcome by order, the Rainbow Serpent embodies the dynamic balance that sustains life. It is not defeated by heroes or confined by gods but continues to move through the landscape, its influence visible in every rainbow, present in every permanent spring. The serpent's role as both creator and law-enforcer reflects the Aboriginal understanding that creation is not a completed act but an ongoing process requiring constant attention and respect.

The mythology collides sharply with modern realities facing Aboriginal communities. When mining companies seek to blast through sacred sites for iron ore extraction, they're essentially proposing to dynamite the Rainbow Serpent's body for profit. The 2020 destruction of Juukan Gorge, a 46,000-year-old Aboriginal heritage site in Western Australia, was blown up by Rio Tinto for access to iron ore worth roughly $135 million. The Puutu Kunti Kurrama and Pinikura peoples had tried to prevent the destruction, but mining rights trumped sacred law. In the Rainbow Serpent's moral universe, such acts would trigger catastrophic punishment; in the modern legal system, they triggered a parliamentary inquiry and some strongly worded letters.

Land rights battles continue to pit ancient law against colonial property concepts. When Aboriginal communities fight for native title over traditional lands, they're arguing that the Rainbow Serpent's creative acts establish legal ownership that predates any European document. The irony is stark: the very legal system that demands written proof of ownership is being asked to recognize laws written in landscape by a serpent's movement through the Dreamtime. It's like asking someone to produce a receipt for the sunrise.

The ongoing struggle for cultural heritage protection reveals the gap between Aboriginal and Western worldviews. To mining executives, Uluru is a large rock with tourist potential and possible mineral deposits. To the Anangu people, it's a sacred site where ancestral beings, including serpent figures, shaped the landscape and established law. When tourists climb Uluru despite requests not to, they're essentially ignoring a "No Trespassing" sign written by the Rainbow Serpent in stone and song.

In a world increasingly disconnected from natural rhythms and ecological realities, the Rainbow Serpent's message carries particular urgency. This mythology is, in fact, a sophisticated environmental philosophy that teaches respect for natural resources, understanding of ecological interconnection, and recognition that human actions have consequences throughout the entire web of existence. The great serpent's gift of water and life comes with clear conditions: respect the land and follow the laws that govern all living relationships.

The serpent's environmental warnings seem prophetic when viewed against contemporary climate change and ecological destruction. Droughts, floods, and extreme weather events that Aboriginal elders might once have attributed to the Rainbow Serpent's displeasure now have scientific explanations involving carbon emissions and planetary heating. Yet the practical result is identical: human actions that disrespect natural balance bring consequences that reshape the landscape and threaten survival.

After all, as any Aboriginal elder might observe with a knowing smile, you wouldn't want to disturb a creature capable of reshaping continents. The Rainbow Serpent is still traveling, still watching, still ready to remind the careless that some things remain sacred, no matter how much the world around them changes. Whether you call it mythology or environmental science, the message remains the same: respect the water, protect the land, or face the consequences of a very annoyed serpent with a long memory and unlimited power to make its displeasure known.

Did You Know?

The Rainbow Serpent's creative and destructive power is mirrored in serpent myths around the world. In Norse mythology, the World Serpent, Jörmungandr, encircles the entire earth, holding it together by biting its own tail, a symbol of eternity. Similarly, the Hindu serpent Ananta, or "the endless," holds the universe on its coils. In these stories, like with the Rainbow Serpent, the serpent isn't a simple monster, but a fundamental force of nature that can both create and destroy.

Through the Looking Glass, A Brief History of Magnification

Rome, 100 AD. A scholar holds a clear glass sphere filled with water over his manuscript, watching in amazement as the tiny letters suddenly double in size. He has no idea he's discovered one of humanity's most useful tools. The magnifying glass had arrived, though it would take another thousand years for anyone to figure out what to do with it.

The Romans knew glass could bend light, they'd been accidentally starting fires with crystal spheres for generations. Pliny the Elder wrote about physicians using glass globes filled with water to cauterize wounds, turning sunlight into a surgical laser. Aristophanes had joked about "burning lenses" sold in Athenian markets as early as 424 BC, proving that even ancient Greeks understood the entertainment value of setting things on fire with focused sunlight. The magnifying glass began its career as humanity's first attempt at weaponizing sunshine.

See Clearly Now

Medieval monks discovered that salvation came in the form of small hemispheric pieces of glass called reading stones. These weren't magnifying glasses as we know them but simple glass bumps that could be placed directly on text to enlarge the letters. For scholars whose livelihood depended on copying manuscripts by candlelight, these reading stones were the difference between productive old age and early retirement. The irony was perfect: in an age when most people believed blindness was divine punishment for sin, monks were using science to keep reading holy books.

Medieval optical theory was a mixture of Greek philosophy, Islamic science, and educated guessing. Light was thought to emerge from the eye rather than enter it, which made explaining magnification about as straightforward as describing color to someone who'd never seen it. The prevailing wisdom held that vision worked like Superman's X-ray vision, with mysterious rays shooting out of the eyeballs to illuminate objects. Under this theory, magnifying glasses presumably worked by making those eye-rays more concentrated, though nobody bothered to explain why only certain pieces of glass possessed this ray-focusing ability.

Enter Roger Bacon, a 13th-century English friar who combined scientific curiosity with medieval England's version of a home laboratory. Around 1250, Bacon began systematically experimenting with convex lenses, documenting how different curvatures produced different levels of magnification. His breakthrough came when he realized that a properly shaped lens could help "old men read small letters again," essentially inventing the world's first anti-aging treatment that actually worked.

Bacon's contribution wasn't the invention of the lens but the methodical study of how lenses worked. He had access to translated works by Ibn al-Haytham, the brilliant Arab polymath who had written about optics in 1021. Al-Haytham's Book of Optics described using convex lenses for magnification, but his work had remained largely unknown in Europe until translations appeared in the 12th century. Medieval science was essentially an elaborate game of telephone played across centuries and continents, with crucial discoveries getting lost in translation, rediscovered, and credited to whoever happened to be writing in the currently fashionable language.

The magnifying glass's real breakthrough came when someone had the brilliant idea to mount two lenses in a frame that could rest on the nose. By the 1280s, Italian craftsmen were producing the world's first eyeglasses, converting handheld magnifiers into hands-free vision correction. The transformation was immediate: scribes could work longer, jewelers could craft finer details, and scholars could read without developing permanent squints. Suddenly, aging didn't automatically disqualify you from intellectual work, a development that must have horrified ambitious young scholars who'd been counting on their elders to gracefully bow out of academic competition.

From Parlor Trick to Scientific Revolution

The magnifying glass's true legacy lay not in what it revealed but in what it made possible. By the late 16th century, Dutch lens-makers had discovered that combining multiple lenses could magnify objects far beyond what single lenses achieved. The Janssen family created the first compound microscope around 1590, while Hans Lipperhey developed the telescope in 1608. What had started as a Roman curiosity for reading small text had evolved into instruments capable of revealing both the infinitely small and the unimaginably distant.

Galileo heard about the Dutch telescope and improved the design within months, turning a novelty into the instrument that would revolutionize astronomy. Anton van Leeuwenhoek pushed magnification in the opposite direction, crafting tiny single lenses so powerful they revealed bacteria, sperm cells, and an entire microscopic world that nobody had imagined existed. The progression was beautifully symmetrical: humanity used the same basic technology to discover that the universe was both far larger and far smaller than anyone had suspected.

The magnifying glass launched the Great Revelation, the centuries-long process of discovering that reality was nothing like what it appeared to be. Telescopes revealed that Earth wasn't the center of anything, microscopes showed that life existed at scales invisible to human perception, and cameras eventually proved that human memory was unreliable. The humble reading stone had grown up to become humanity's most effective tool for destroying comfortable illusions about our place in the cosmos.

Today's magnifying glasses remain fundamentally unchanged from Roger Bacon's medieval experiments, a testament to the elegance of the original design. Watch repairers still use jeweler's loupes, detectives carry pocket magnifiers, and children explore their backyards with plastic lenses that work on the same principles discovered by Roman water-gazers. Digital technology has replicated magnification through software, but the physical lens retains its appeal, because there's something satisfying about using a tool that has remained fundamentally unchanged for eight centuries.

The magnifying glass emoji remains the universal symbol for search and investigation, proving that some innovations become so fundamental they transcend their original technology. Through this simple piece of curved glass, we learned to read the fine print of nature itself. The magnifying glass didn't just make small things larger; it made the invisible visible and transformed human curiosity into systematic discovery.

Did You Know?

The first telescope was so unimpressive that Hans Lipperhey failed to get a patent because Dutch officials argued anyone could easily make one. Like the magnifying glass before it, revolutionary optical tools often look deceptively simple until someone realizes their potential.

Hippolyte Bayard created photography's first artistic protest in 1840 by posing as a drowned corpse, bitter that Daguerre got credit for inventing photography first. His camera used the same lens principles that Roger Bacon studied with magnifying glasses, proving that optical discoveries have always triggered fierce competition over recognition.

The Hubble Space Telescope's flawed mirror was fixed with tiny corrective mirrors that essentially gave it "space glasses." The solution used the same basic principle as medieval reading stones - adding more curved glass to compensate for imperfect vision.

Modern camera lenses descended directly from magnifying glasses, using curved glass to focus light just like Roman scholars with their water-filled spheres. The difference is that cameras capture what the lens sees permanently, while those ancient Romans could only marvel at the temporary enlargement of their manuscripts.

The Quartermaster's Vote, How Thieves Beat Kings at Governance

Nassau, 1717. The morning sun cuts through harbor mist as two dozen men circle a pile of Spanish silver on the sand. Voices rise, hands gesture at the glittering coins. Then someone calls for a vote. Twenty-four hands shoot up, six stay down. The prize gets split equally, minus shares for the ship's fund. No royal decree, no noble bloodline, no ancient privilege decides the matter. Just voices counted under a black flag.

New Providence Island sits 180 miles southeast of Florida, a limestone speck in the Bahamas with a natural harbor perfect for careening ships. Twenty-one miles long, seven miles wide, roughly the size of Manhattan if Manhattan were populated entirely by armed tax evaders. The harbor's shallow waters kept large British warships out while welcoming the swift, shallow-draft sloops pirates preferred. The Pirate Republic of Nassau at its peak held a thousand outlaws governing themselves on this spit of Bahamian sand, writing democracy in gunpowder and gold. For a brief, chaotic decade, these sea rovers built a functioning society based on consent of the governed, elected leadership, and written law. They called it brotherhood. History might call it America's rough draft.

Democracy at Gunpoint

Walk into any Nassau tavern in 1717 and you'll find paper nailed to the wall, ink-stained and salt-crusted but perfectly legible. These pirate codes weren't romantic fiction but practical governance documents that accidentally invented the democratic institutions we take for granted today. Every crew drafted their own before each voyage, hammering out the basics in ship's councils. Equal shares, democratic votes, worker's compensation.

Pirates created progressive labor practices two centuries before legitimate governments caught up. A common distribution split gave each crew member one share, the quartermaster 1.25 shares, the captain maybe 1.5 or 2. Merchant vessels saw captains claim ten times a sailor's wage; Royal Navy ships had admirals living like kings while crew ate maggoty bread. Pirates flattened the hierarchy into something Scandinavians would later call social democracy, minus the healthcare and plus the cannons.

Their injury compensation system would make modern socialist parties weep with envy. Lose a right arm in battle, collect 600 Spanish dollars. Left arm, 500. Eye or finger, 100. These weren't insurance policies sold by London brokers but collective agreements funded by shared plunder. When Blackbeard's quartermaster Israel Hands caught a musket ball in the knee and was permanently crippled, he wasn't abandoned to starve. Instead, he was given shore leave in Bath, North Carolina, to recuperate while still drawing

110

from the crew's resources. Hands survived Blackbeard's final battle precisely because pirate society cared for its wounded rather than discarding them.

Pirates invented checks and balances decades before Montesquieu theorized about separation of powers. They split authority to prevent any one person from holding absolute control, the same principle that would later shape the U.S. Constitution. The real power aboard pirate ships rested not with captains but quartermasters, elected representatives who controlled daily operations, settled disputes, and distributed loot. Benjamin Hornigold might have been captain of the *Ranger*, but his quartermaster held the crew's proxy to overrule him on everything except combat tactics.

These outlaws practiced direct democracy while Europe still bowed to divine right. Attack that Spanish galleon? Put it to a vote. Change course for Charleston? Count hands. Even punishments required crew approval. The code of Captain John Phillips specified that theft from shipmates earned 40 lashes or marooning, but only after "being brought before the company." No star chambers, no royal prerogative, just trial by jury of your peers.

Pirates perfected accountability in leadership when kings claimed divine authority. Captains could be "turned out" by majority vote for cowardice, cruelty, or simple incompetence. Bartholomew Roberts got deposed twice before finding a crew that stuck with him. Royal Navy captains held commission from the crown and answered to no common sailor, regardless of performance.

Blackbeard's Leadership Seminar

Benjamin Hornigold understood the political game better than most. Operating from Nassau between 1715 and 1717, he mentored a generation of pirate captains including Edward Teach and "Calico" Jack Rackham. But Hornigold was a patriot underneath his black flag, targeting only Spanish and French vessels while carefully avoiding British ships. When the crown offered amnesty in 1718, he jumped at the chance, trading his captaincy for a commission as pirate hunter.

His student Teach took a different path. As Blackbeard, he perfected unconventional strategy wrapped in theatrical terror. When he blockaded Charleston harbor for a week in 1718, he wasn't after gold or Spanish silver. He demanded a chest of medicine for his crew, bringing commerce to a standstill until the colony's leaders delivered basic medical supplies. Hemp fibers woven through his beard and lit before battle created a demonic cloud around his face, but behind the performance lay shrewd political calculation. Blackbeard preferred surrender to slaughter because dead crews told no tales, spread no legends. His fearsome reputation was psychological warfare, carefully cultivated to minimize actual violence while maximizing practical results.

The Nassau brotherhood also produced history's most famous female pirates. Anne Bonny and Mary Read sailed with Rackham in 1720. Their presence aboard ship challenges easy assumptions about pirate society. These weren't women disguised as men but openly female crew members who fought, voted, and shared equally in prize money. When Rackham's crew faced trial in Jamaica, witnesses testified that Bonny and Read "wore men's jackets, and long trousers, and handkerchiefs tied about their heads, and each of them had a machete and pistol in their hands." They had earned their place through competence, not birth or gender.

Nassau's success rested on perfect timing and geography. The Treaty of Utrecht ended the War of Spanish Succession in 1713, creating a massive labor shock as thousands of unemployed privateers flooded Caribbean markets. These men knew ships, navigation, and naval combat, but peace offered them only merchant wages or naval impressment. Piracy provided a third option. Worker ownership of the means of production, 18th-century style.

A successful cruise might net each crew member £1,000 in prize money, equivalent to twenty years' wages for a London laborer. Even accounting for the risk of hanging, piracy offered the best expected return available to working-class men in the Atlantic world. Nassau became a boom town powered by redistributed Spanish silver, hosting a thousand residents at its peak.

The island's economy ran on more than plunder. Merchants arrived regularly from Charleston, New York, and Philadelphia to buy stolen goods at deep discounts, turning pirate raids into a parallel trading network. This merchant complicity transformed Nassau from a criminal hideout into a functioning commercial hub where stolen cargo got laundered into legitimate trade.

The social mix was equally radical. Pirate crews welcomed escaped slaves, runaway servants, and naval deserters without regard for background. Samuel "Black Sam" Bellamy's crew included at least 30 men of African descent, while Blackbeard's quartermaster was a formerly enslaved man named Caesar. Aboard ship, previous status mattered less than current contribution. Rough meritocracy, enforced by the democratic process.

Bellamy earned his nickname for his democratic leadership style and habit of freeing captured crews rather than killing them. He was essentially running a floating HR department where the policy was "nobody dies unless absolutely necessary." When his ship Whydah Gally sank in a storm off Cape Cod in 1717, it took down one of the most successful pirate vessels and its most progressive captain. The ocean, apparently, was less impressed with workplace equality than historians would later be.

Death by Paperwork

London's response came in 1718 with the appointment of Woodes Rogers as royal governor. Rogers himself was a former privateer who understood how pirates thought: their fierce independence, their distrust of authority, and their focus on immediate profit over long-term planning. Rather than attacking Nassau directly, he offered the King's Pardon to any pirate who surrendered by September 1718. The strategy split the brotherhood cleanly. Pragmatists like Hornigold accepted amnesty while hardliners like Teach and Charles Vane rejected it.

Rogers then deployed the ultimate divide-and-conquer tactic. He commissioned former pirates like Hornigold to hunt down their old comrades who refused the pardon. The brotherhood found itself literally at war with itself as yesterday's allies became today's bounty hunters. Meanwhile, Rogers implemented economic warfare, blockading Nassau harbor and cutting supply lines. Pirates needed food, water, gunpowder, and ship repair facilities. By controlling access to these necessities, Rogers made the pirate life unsustainable without firing a shot.

The Pirate Republic's greatest strength became its fatal weakness. The same democratic individualism that made them progressive prevented unified resistance to Rogers. Without a central government or single leader, each crew made separate deals or separate stands. The endgame played out across 1718 and 1719. Blackbeard fell to Royal Navy Lieutenant Robert Maynard off the North Carolina coast, shot five times and slashed twenty before dropping. Vane was captured in Jamaica and hanged. Rackham's crew, including Bonny and Read, met the gallows in Spanish Town. By 1720, the Pirate Republic existed only in memory and maritime law.

Code Still Loading

Pirates didn't invent democracy. Greeks voted in their city assemblies, Romans elected senators, and medieval Icelanders gathered in open-air parliaments where any free man could speak his mind. But Nassau's experiment stands apart because it came from desperate need, not noble ideas. When violent criminals accidentally build better worker protections than modern tech companies, when thieves and murderers create fairer pay than Silicon Valley, you're witnessing something fundamental about how humans actually organize themselves.

Pirates proved that democratic institutions aren't fragile flowers requiring centuries of cultivation. They're just how humans actually organize themselves when survival depends on cooperation. The Nassau codes weren't inspired by Aristotle or John Locke's treatises on government by consent but by the simple problem of keeping violent men working together on a wooden ship surrounded by sharks. Strip away the philosophical theories and constitutional conventions, and you find the same basic solutions emerging wherever people need to make collective decisions under pressure.

The digital age keeps rediscovering pirate principles. Bitcoin operates on distributed consensus rather than central banking, with thousands of computers collectively validating transactions instead of trusting a single authority. It's essentially Blackbeard's crew voting on whether to accept that Spanish silver, except now the crew spans continents and the silver is digital. Open-source software relies on volunteer collaboration. Worker-owned cooperatives flatten corporate hierarchies. Each follows the same insight that drove Nassau's golden age. Legitimate authority flows from the consent of the governed, not hereditary privilege or institutional decree.

The methods have evolved but the rebellion continues. Every startup that distributes equity broadly, every union that demands worker representation, every community that writes its own rules carries a trace of Nassau's DNA. When your neighborhood Bitcoin meetup splits the bill equally or your open-source project votes on code changes, you're channeling 18th-century quartermasters counting hands on a Nassau beach. The black flag may be furled, but the ballot remains rough, ready, and effective.

On Nassau's abandoned quay, salt wind still rattles the occasional scrap of paper against weathered posts. Sometimes the words are still legible. "Every man has a vote." Three centuries later, the count continues.

Did You Know?

Switzerland didn't grant women the right to vote until 1971, making it one of the last Western democracies to do so. Meanwhile, Anne Bonny and Mary Read were voting on pirate ship business in 1720, showing that democratic inclusion often happens faster on the margins than in the mainstream.

Modern corporate shareholder democracy typically gives voting power based on ownership stakes, while pirate crews gave every member equal votes regardless of investment. Contemporary worker cooperatives use the same "one member, one vote" system that Nassau's quartermasters pioneered.

Doctor Feelgood, The Art of Feeling Better Without Getting Well

"Doctor Feelgood" sounds like a compliment until you think about it. The phrase describes someone who makes you feel good whether you're sick or not, which means they're either unnecessary or dangerous. In modern slang, it's your dealer, your enabler, your wellness influencer promising transformation through supplements. Everyone pays, everyone feels better temporarily, and everyone discovers that feeling good isn't the same as being well.

The term carries swagger from rock and roll, where bands like Mötley Crüe turned it into an anthem for excess. But its origins lie in examination rooms and bunkers, where real doctors crossed ethical lines to keep powerful people performing. From Hitler's physician to JFK's "miracle shot" specialist, the story of Doctor Feelgood reveals how the promise of easy fixes corrupts both medicine and the people who seek shortcuts to wellness. It's snake oil with a medical degree, selling the same ancient promise that there's always a bottle, shot, or pill that can make everything better.

The Führer's Pharmacy

Theodor Morell was the perfect Doctor Feelgood: a cartoonishly plump physician with stale body odor and theatrical confidence who convinced the most powerful man in Europe to become his personal chemistry experiment. Albert Speer famously described him as "a pig in a chemist's shop," and the comparison was apt. Morell carried himself with the showman's swagger of a carnival barker, his medical bag packed with an eclectic arsenal of experimental compounds, animal extracts, and untested substances that would horrify modern physicians.

Between 1936 and 1945, this unhygienic quack transformed Hitler from an anxious hypochondriac into a manic dictator through pharmaceutical wizardry. The word "quack" comes from "quacksalver," Dutch for someone who quacks loudly about their salves and potions. Like ducks making noise by the pond, these fake doctors made lots of noise about miracle cures. His daily regimen included methamphetamines (Pervitin) for energy, opioids (Eukodal) for pain and euphoria, and a rotating cast of vitamins, glucose, and bizarre animal organ extracts. But Morell's true genius lay in his obsession with injections, believing they were the most efficient delivery system for his "miracle" cures.

Morell's briefcase was a traveling pharmacy of the absurd. He injected Hitler with hormones from animal testicles, pancreases, and livers. These extracts were supposed to restore youthful energy. His most infamous mixture was Mutaflor. This was gut bacteria taken from a Bulgarian peasant and grown in a lab. Morell shot it into Hitler's veins to treat stomach problems. Beyond the core stimulants and painkillers, he pushed experimental compounds. These drugs had never been tested on humans. He turned the Führer into a human guinea pig.

The transformation was dramatic. Hitler became increasingly animated and decisive after his sessions with Morell. He displayed frenzied confidence that powered his early military successes. But Morell's records tell the real story. Allied forces found them after the war. They document over 1,100 injections throughout their relationship. By 1944, Hitler required multiple daily shots just to function. His body shook without chemical support.

Morell's presence in the bunker during the war's final days wasn't loyalty but necessity. He spent those last months adjusting drug doses. His patient's mental state was falling apart. Morell was a disheveled figure maintaining his pharmaceutical hold over a crumbling dictator.

The doctor who promised to restore the Führer's health had instead turned him into a walking pharmacy. Hitler was dependent on chemicals for basic emotional stability. Morell survived the war but not his reputation.

American forces captured him on May 21, 1945, near Hitler's final headquarters. Allied intelligence officers thought he might be a major Nazi conspirator or poison expert. They held him at an internment camp near Dachau for two years. His interrogators were more interested in politics than his medical practices. His notebooks detailed every injection he gave Hitler. These became key sources for historians. But his captors weren't impressed. His answers were rambling, unhelpful, and full of self-pity.

The imprisonment destroyed Morell's health. The man who promised to cure the Führer couldn't heal himself. He suffered from severe nervous disorders.

His physical health collapsed rapidly. He was transferred from prison to a hospital in Bavaria. He died on May 26, 1948, just over three years after his capture. The cause of death wasn't widely publicized.

Morell's downfall followed a familiar pattern among history's drug-dispensing doctors. From Freud with his cocaine experiments to countless physicians who "tested" their own prescriptions, many practitioners became their own best customers. They convinced themselves that regular sampling was scientific research rather than addiction. Morell likely believed his own pharmaceutical propaganda until his supply ran out. His final years were marked by a lack of the feelgood tonics he had freely given others. He died sick, alone, and without his cache of potions. The ultimate irony for history's most notorious feelgood practitioner.

American Miracle Shots

Max Jacobson brought the Doctor Feelgood concept to American high society with more polish but equal recklessness. Throughout the 1950s and 1960s, this Austrian-born physician built a practice around "vitamin shots" that made celebrities and politicians feel superhuman. His patient list read like a who's who of American power, including President John F. Kennedy, who used Jacobson's injections to manage chronic back pain and the demands of the presidency.

Jacobson's "miracle shots" contained amphetamines, vitamins, steroids, and animal organ extracts mixed in proportions he adjusted according to each patient's needs and tolerance. Clients reported feeling euphoric, energetic, and mentally sharp for hours after injection. Broadway performers used them to get through grueling show schedules. Politicians relied on them for campaign energy. Socialites treated them as luxury health maintenance.

The appeal lay in Jacobson's presentation as much as his chemistry. Unlike street dealers or obvious quacks, he maintained a legitimate medical practice with impressive credentials. He had studied at German universities and published research on tissue therapy. His Park Avenue office suggested respectability, while his willingness to make house calls demonstrated personal service that wealthy patients expected.

Kennedy's dependence on Jacobson's treatments became particularly problematic during international crises. The president received injections before major speeches, important meetings, and foreign travel. Secret Service agents worried about their commander-in-chief's reliance on an unregulated drug cocktail during moments requiring clear judgment. When Attorney General Robert Kennedy tried to have the injections analyzed, the president reportedly replied, "I don't care if it's horse piss. It works."

Jacobson's downfall came in 1970 when federal investigators discovered he was using non-FDA-approved substances and operating without proper oversight. The New York State Board of Health found that his "vitamin shots" contained dangerous levels of amphetamines and other controlled substances. His medical license was revoked, but not before he had demonstrated how easily the promise of enhanced performance could corrupt medical practice.

The Wellness Industrial Complex

The modern Doctor Feelgood operates through Instagram accounts and wellness conferences rather than black medical bags. The basic transaction remains unchanged. Today's practitioners sell the feeling of health through supplements, lifestyle programs, and therapeutic experiences. They promise transformation without the inconvenience of actual medical diagnosis or treatment.

Gwyneth Paltrow's Goop perfected this model. The lifestyle brand built a multi-million-dollar empire selling jade "yoni eggs" that supposedly improved sexual energy and balanced hormones. Yes, you read that correctly: rocks for your reproductive organs, marketed at the same price point as a decent dinner. California prosecutors forced the company to pay $145,000 in civil penalties for making unproven health claims, which probably covered about three weeks of Goop's jade egg sales. The company also promoted vaginal steaming and coffee enemas, treatments that medical professionals call dangerous and useless. We've officially reached the point where someone can become a wellness guru by suggesting people put coffee where coffee was never meant to go. The brand sells empowerment and well-being through products with no scientific basis, proving that if you package absurdity in enough lifestyle branding, people will literally buy anything.

Wellness influencers have mastered the art of selling solutions to problems their followers didn't know they had. They promote "adrenal support" supplements for tiredness that might actually be sleep disorders. They push "detox" programs for symptoms that could signal real illness. They offer "mood-boosting" protocols that bypass actual mental health care. The appeal lies in skipping doctors entirely. Direct access to feeling better without the complexity of genuine healthcare.

The placebo effect provides scientific cover for much of this industry. A placebo is when people feel better even though the treatment does nothing medically. People genuinely improve after starting new supplement routines or wellness programs. This happens regardless of whether the treatments actually work. Customer satisfaction validates the provider's methods. The improvements often come from attention, expectation, and lifestyle changes rather than the specific products being sold.

Corporate wellness programs represent the institutional version of Doctor Feelgood services. Companies like Google and Microsoft invest in meditation apps, on-site massage, and stress management seminars. These make employees feel cared for without addressing real issues like overwork, bad management, or low pay. The programs succeed by making people feel better about situations that actually need systemic change. It's cheaper to buy everyone a mindfulness app than to hire more staff.

Quick Fixes and Slow Bills

After World War II, American forces captured German drug research, including Morell's detailed studies on methamphetamine and pain management. The same stimulants that kept Hitler functional in his bunker became the foundation for modern ADHD medications. OxyContin shares chemical similarities with the Eukodal that Morell administered to the Führer. Sometimes the real medicine and the fake medicine end up in the same place.

The opioid crisis reveals how legitimate medicine drifts into Doctor Feelgood territory. Purdue Pharma aggressively marketed OxyContin in the 1990s, claiming the drug was non-addictive. Sales representatives received large bonuses to push the drug on doctors for a wide range of pain conditions. The "feelgood" of initial pain relief came at the ultimate price. Economic incentives corrupted legitimate medicine, turning prescription pads into tools for a business model that caused immense suffering.

The hidden cost emerges over time. Morell's patients developed tolerance requiring ever-increasing doses. Jacobson's clients found their enhanced performance dependent on regular injections. Modern wellness consumers discover their supplement regimens become expensive habits that interfere with addressing real problems.

The ethical boundary lies in honesty about what's being sold. Legitimate practitioners acknowledge uncertainty and discuss risks. Doctor Feelgood providers promise certainty, minimize risks, and sell the feeling of being helped rather than actual help.

Whether delivered through syringes or social media, the appeal remains constant. Feeling better now rather than getting better eventually. From ancient snake oil salesmen to Nazi bunkers to Beverly Hills clinics, every era produces its Doctor Feelgood promising easy answers to hard problems. The prescription for avoiding them may be the most uncomfortable medicine of all: accepting that real health requires patience, effort, and sometimes feeling worse before feeling better. Unlike the shortcuts that promise to make everything better, this approach actually works.

Did You Know?

Theranos founder Elizabeth Holmes convinced investors to pour $945 million into fake blood testing technology by using a single drop of blood for tests that actually required vials. Like Morell's miracle injections, the appeal was bypassing uncomfortable medical realities - in this case, the inconvenience of normal blood draws.

The Prime Minister's Proof, Churchill's Liquid Schedule

"I may be drunk, Miss,

but in the morning, I will be sober and you will still be ugly."

Churchill allegedly delivered this retort to Lady Astor during a heated parliamentary exchange, though the quote's authenticity remains disputed. Whether he actually said it or not, the line captures Churchill's reputation for quick wit fueled by constant alcohol consumption. His drinking wasn't a secret vice but a public aspect of his persona, as carefully managed as his speeches and as integral to his image as his cigars.

If Winston Churchill were applying for jobs today, his resume would read "Functioning Alcoholic, World-Class." He operated on a schedule that would hospitalize most people within a week. From his morning "mouthful of alcohol in a tumbler of soda" to his 3 AM whiskey nightcaps, Britain's wartime leader maintained what might be history's most meticulously structured drinking routine. This wasn't the chaotic consumption of a typical alcoholic but a precisely calibrated system that fueled one of the 20th century's most demanding careers. Churchill didn't just drink heavily; he drank systematically, turning alcohol consumption into a form of performance enhancement that somehow sustained rather than destroyed his legendary productivity.

The Clockwork of Consumption

Churchill's day began at 9 AM with what he called his "morning wake-up": a small tumbler containing a mouthful of whiskey or sherry topped with soda water. By 10 AM, he had settled into his most intensive work period, accompanied by the famous "Churchill polly": a tall glass of heavily diluted Johnnie Walker Black Label and soda that remained at his elbow through three hours of dictation, correspondence, and strategic planning.

Lunch at 1 PM marked the day's first major escalation: a full imperial pint of Pol Roger champagne, roughly 20 ounces consumed over the course of his meal. Churchill maintained an exclusive relationship with this particular brand, once telling Madame Pol Roger that her champagne was "the only thing that never disappointed him." When Madame Pol Roger died, he ordered black-bordered labels for his bottles in her honor.

The afternoon transition came at 3 PM with a glass of cognac, serving as prelude to his non-negotiable daily nap. This wasn't recreational drinking but functional: the cognac marked his shift from morning intensity to afternoon recovery, allowing him to recharge for the evening's work.

Dinner at 8 PM brought another imperial pint of champagne, consumed during his famously lengthy evening meals that doubled as informal cabinet meetings.

The late-night hours, from dinner until his typical 3 AM bedtime, saw a return to whiskey and soda supplemented by brandy or additional cognac.

Churchill famously declared, "I have taken more out of alcohol than alcohol has taken out of me," and dismissed critics with his quip that "water is for washing." His approach to alcohol was as methodical as his approach to warfare: precise timing, consistent quantities, and unwavering discipline. Most alcoholics lose control of their routine; Churchill turned routine into his form of control. The total daily consumption approached what modern medicine would consider a lethal routine: approximately six to eight glasses of whiskey and soda, two imperial pints of champagne, and several glasses of cognac or brandy.

The Functional Alcoholic's Paradox

Churchill's drinking defied typical patterns of alcohol dependency because it served function over intoxication. His biographers consistently note that he rarely appeared drunk despite consuming quantities that would incapacitate most people. The key lay in his systematic approach: highly diluted drinks, constant food intake, and carefully timed consumption that allowed his body to metabolize alcohol throughout the day rather than in sharp peaks.

His drinking functioned as a powerful diplomatic weapon. Churchill deliberately used his extraordinary tolerance to psychological advantage, often drinking visiting dignitaries under the table during crucial negotiations. Stalin reportedly once complained that Churchill's capacity made their meetings exhausting, while American officials learned to pace themselves carefully during extended sessions with the Prime Minister.

This routine fueled remarkable productivity during Britain's darkest hour. Between 1940 and 1945, while maintaining his drinking schedule, Churchill delivered over 300 speeches to Parliament, wrote dozens of strategic memoranda, conducted thousands of hours of diplomatic meetings, and personally oversaw military operations across three continents.

He dictated his six-volume memoir "The Second World War" during late-night sessions and won the Nobel Prize for Literature in 1953. Notably, Churchill didn't win the Nobel Peace Prize despite ending the world's greatest war, nor the Prize for Medicine despite pioneering new frontiers in liver function. The Swedish Academy honored him specifically for his "mastery of historical and biographical description as well as for brilliant oratory," proving that whiskey-fueled eloquence counts as high literature.

His alcohol-fueled nocturnal work sessions produced iconic speeches including "We shall fight on the beaches" and "Their finest hour," which he often composed while sipping whiskey and pacing his study until dawn.

This routine represented a form of self-medication for the immense pressures of his role, particularly during World War II when Britain's survival often depended on his decision-making. The alcohol helped manage what Churchill called his "black dog" of depression while maintaining the manic energy required for 18-hour workdays.

His personal physician, Lord Moran, remained largely unconcerned by Churchill's consumption, reflecting the era's very different medical understanding of alcohol's effects. Moran viewed Churchill's drinking as part of his exceptional constitution rather than a health risk, an attitude that would be considered medical malpractice today but demonstrates how drastically perspectives on alcohol have shifted.

The routine created a myth of invincibility that served Britain's wartime morale. Citizens facing rationing and bombing took inspiration from a leader who seemed to operate on superhuman scales in everything from alcohol consumption to work output. Churchill's drinking became visible proof that British leadership possessed the extraordinary constitution required to outlast Nazi Germany.

Yet this same routine revealed the personal cost of such demanding leadership. The alcohol masked chronic stress, irregular sleep, and the psychological weight of making decisions that affected millions of lives. Churchill's drinking was simultaneously his greatest strength and his most dangerous vulnerability.

Churchill's routine was sustainable only due to exceptional genetics, constant medical attention, and circumstances that would destroy most people regardless of their alcohol tolerance. His drinking pattern worked for Churchill specifically, in his particular historical moment, but represents a cautionary tale rather than a model for leadership.

Like his famous retort to Lady Astor, Churchill's relationship with alcohol was carefully crafted performance art. His drinking wasn't a secret vice but a public demonstration of superhuman constitution. The man who claimed "I may be drunk, Miss, but in the morning I will be sober and you will still be ugly" built his entire persona around controlled excess. Yet even history's most functional alcoholic operated despite his dependencies rather than because of them, proving that exceptional performance and severe substance dependency can coexist but should never be confused as cause and effect. If Churchill were applying for jobs today, his resume would indeed read "Functioning Alcoholic, World-Class," but the emphasis should remain firmly on the cautionary "alcoholic" rather than the impressive "world-class."

Black Blizzard Country, When the Prairie Took Flight

April 14, 1935. Noon turned to midnight across the Great Plains as a wall of dust two miles high rolled east from the Texas Panhandle. In Dodge City, Kansas, the Folkers family watched from their kitchen window as the black blizzard swallowed the horizon. Mrs. Folkers wet dish towels and pressed them against the window frames while her husband nailed blankets over the door. By evening, flour-fine dust coated every surface inside their sealed house, and each breath tasted of grit and grass roots torn from soil that had once held the prairie together.

The Dust Bowl wasn't just bad weather but the collision between human ambition and natural limits. Farmers had spent two decades proving they could make the desert bloom. Unfortunately, they made it fly instead.

130

The Great Plow-Up

Between 1914 and 1919, world war drove wheat prices to unprecedented heights. A bushel that sold for 80 cents in 1914 brought $2.19 by 1919, transforming prairie sod from worthless grassland into potential gold mines. Land promoters, government officials, and even scientists promoted the theory that "rain follows the plow," claiming intensive farming would increase regional precipitation. Above-average rainfall in the 1920s gave farmers false confidence that the climate was permanently changing.

The Enlarged Homestead Act of 1909 opened millions of acres of marginal land to settlement. During the "Great Plow-Up," farmers tilled 5.2 million acres of additional grassland between 1925 and 1930 alone, an area nearly seven times the size of Rhode Island. Steam tractors could destroy in an afternoon what had taken grass millennia to build. The International Harvester Company sold 4,000 tractors in western Kansas alone during 1926, each capable of breaking 50 acres of sod per day.

Farmers planted wheat in straight furrows across rolling terrain, creating channels for erosion. They removed the native buffalo grass, grama grass, and bluestem that had survived ice ages and centuries of drought by sending roots down 15 feet to find moisture. The Great Plains soil was particularly vulnerable: fine, loess-based particles that pulverized easily and lifted in wind, unlike the coarser, heavier soil found elsewhere.

Prairie grasses covered soil with a thick mat that could withstand winds exceeding 60 miles per hour. Wheat stubble provided minimal protection, and fallow fields offered none. When farmers plowed their fields each fall, they created loose, pulverized soil with no plant cover, exposed to constant Plains wind.

When the Sky Fell and Washington Listened

The drought began in 1931 and intensified through 1936. Strong spring winds lifted fine particles from bare fields, creating static electricity so intense it could short out car engines, cause sparks between people shaking hands, and knock a person off their feet. These dust clouds could rise to 10,000 feet and travel hundreds of miles, depositing Plains topsoil on ships in the Atlantic Ocean.

On April 14, 1935, the largest storm of all rolled across the Plains. Black Sunday's dust wall reached two miles high and moved at 60 miles per hour, carrying 300,000 tons of soil in a single storm system that eventually darkened skies over Washington D.C., Chicago, and New York.

Hugh Hammond Bennett, appointed to lead the Soil Conservation Service in 1935, was testifying before Congress that same day when the Black Sunday storm hit. As dust from the Plains darkened the sky over Washington D.C., he told lawmakers, "This, gentlemen, is what I'm talking about." The dramatic timing secured funding for his agency.

"Dust pneumonia" hospitalized hundreds of people. Dr. John H. Blue of Guymon, Oklahoma, reported treating patients whose lungs contained so much dust that X-rays showed completely opaque chest cavities. The Red Cross distributed thousands of masks to residents who couldn't escape the fine silica particles that penetrated every sealed space.

The Resettlement Administration estimated that 3.5 million people left the Plains states during the 1930s. In California's migrant camps, former wheat farmers picked cotton and fruit for subsistence wages while living in conditions that shocked Depression-era observers.

Bennett mapped soil types across the Plains, identifying which areas could safely support cultivation and which should return to grass. The Civilian Conservation Corps employed 200,000 young men to plant the Prairie States Forestry Project, a 100-mile-wide shelterbelt stretching from North Dakota to the Texas Panhandle. They planted 200 million trees on 30,000 farms.

Contour plowing followed the natural curves of the land, preventing water from carrying topsoil away. Strip cropping alternated wheat with soil-holding crops like sorghum. Farmers learned to leave stubble standing through winter, providing wind protection.

The Agricultural Adjustment Act paid farmers to take marginal land out of production. Soil erosion rates dropped dramatically across the Plains during the late 1930s, even before the drought ended.

Dust and Memory

The institutional memory of the Dust Bowl faded as prosperity returned. During World War II, high grain prices again encouraged farmers to plow marginal land. The 1950s brought another severe drought and dust storms, proving that when it comes to agricultural amnesia, Americans have remarkably consistent memories: they remember the profits and forget the dust. The cycle repeated during the 1970s when Soviet grain purchases drove wheat prices to record levels.

The Ogallala Aquifer, which provides water for 30% of American crop production, is being drained six times faster than it can be recharged naturally. The water is essentially fossil water from the last Ice Age, making modern irrigation the agricultural equivalent of strip-mining dinosaurs. In some areas, the water table has dropped 150 feet since irrigation began.

Climate change adds volatility, with longer droughts punctuated by extreme precipitation events. The frequency of "derecho" windstorms has increased, creating conditions similar to the dust storms of the 1930s when they encounter unprotected soil. Yet regenerative agriculture practices focus on rebuilding soil organic matter through diverse crop rotations, cover crops, and integrated livestock grazing. The Conservation Reserve Program pays farmers to convert highly erodible cropland back to grass, removing 24 million acres from production nationwide.

On a farm near Garden City, Kansas, fourth-generation farmer Jake Tronstad runs dark prairie soil through his fingers, feeling the structure that three decades of conservation tillage and cover crops have restored. His grandfather watched this same soil blow away during the 1930s and spent years rebuilding it. When spring winds rise across the Plains, Tronstad's fields hold fast. The soil that once turned noon to midnight stays where it belongs, anchored by roots and held together by knowledge that land has limits, and exceeding them sends the future blowing away on the wind.

Did You Know?

The Sahara Desert sends 22 million tons of dust to the Amazon rainforest every year, fertilizing South American soil with African minerals. Like the Dust Bowl storms that deposited Great Plains topsoil in the Atlantic, this global dust transport system shows that one continent's erosion becomes another's agricultural foundation.

The largest dust storm ever recorded happened in 2009 when a wall of dust 500 miles wide and 3,000 feet high engulfed Sydney, Australia, turning the sky orange and shutting down the city for hours. Unlike the Dust Bowl's man-made disaster, this was natural desert dust - proving that sometimes nature creates its own version of Black Sunday without any help from farmers.

Devil's Rope, How Barbed Wire Fenced the World

Across the vast plains of the American West, cattle roamed freely through endless grasslands where property lines existed only on paper. Farmers watched helplessly as livestock trampled their crops, while ranchers claimed grazing rights to millions of unfenced acres. The open range seemed eternal until 1873, when Illinois farmer Joseph Glidden twisted two strands of wire together, adding sharp metal barbs at regular intervals. His patent for "The Winner" would close the frontier forever.

Glidden's innovation was brilliantly simple. Cheap steel wire that could keep animals in or out without the expense of wooden fencing. A mile of barbed wire cost just $2 compared to $20 for traditional rail fencing. Within a decade, companies were producing millions of tons annually, and settlers were stringing it across the continent. What had been open range became defined property. Crops grew protected behind wire barriers. Order replaced chaos on the prairie.

Progress came with violence. The Range Wars erupted as cattlemen fought farmers over newly fenced land. Ranchers cut wire fences in nighttime raids while farmers shot trespassers. In Johnson County, Wyoming, hired gunmen murdered homesteaders who dared fence water sources.

Native Americans watched their ancestral hunting grounds carved into parcels, calling the new barrier "the Devil's rope." The Cheyenne and Lakota believed the metal itself was cursed, a supernatural barrier that severed their connection to the land and blocked the ancient buffalo migration routes their ancestors had followed for centuries. To them, the wire represented something more sinister than mere property division. It was a physical manifestation of spiritual disconnection, cutting the threads that bound them to their homeland.

The wire that brought civilization also brought confinement. Anyone who has driven through rural America knows the sight of endless fence lines stretching to the horizon, so commonplace we barely notice them. Yet each strand represents a moment when open land became private property, when the commons became enclosed, when freedom of movement yielded to the logic of ownership.

The Military Discovery

The Boer War of 1899 revealed barbed wire's darker potential. British forces, struggling against guerrilla fighters across the South African veld, strung wire to channel enemy movement and protect supply lines. General Horatio Kitchener discovered its most sinister application by ordering the construction of concentration camps ringed with barbed wire, where Boer women and children were interned to prevent them from aiding the guerrillas.

Over 100,000 civilians were imprisoned behind these wire barriers. Poor sanitation, inadequate food, and disease killed nearly 30,000 people, including 22,000 children. The camps turned Glidden's farming innovation into an instrument of systematic oppression. Barbed wire had evolved from protecting crops to imprisoning human beings.

Military planners worldwide recognized that cheap wire could be more valuable than expensive fortifications. What cost farmers pennies per foot could stop cavalry charges and channel infantry into killing zones. The technology of the ranch had become the technology of war.

World War I transformed barbed wire into the defining feature of modern warfare. Across the Western Front, millions of tons of wire created impenetrable barriers between opposing armies. These weren't simple fence lines but elaborate entanglements with multiple rows of concertina wire, spirals of razor-sharp coils, and trip wires connected to flares and explosives.

Soldiers crossing no man's land faced wire obstacles designed to trap and delay them in machine gun fire. Men became entangled in the coils, hanging helpless between the trenches while enemy bullets found their mark. The wire turned battlefields into slaughterhouses, making traditional cavalry charges obsolete and forcing armies into years of bloody stalemate.

During brutal trench raids, soldiers developed a morbid practice of "tagging" captured enemies. They would deliberately tangle a prisoner in barbed wire, cut off a piece, and twist it around the captive's arm or wrist before dragging them back to their own lines. This ensured the prisoner couldn't escape and added a new level of dehumanization to warfare. The wire that once marked property lines now marked human beings as possessed objects.

Military engineers developed new weapons specifically to defeat wire. Bangalore torpedoes to blast gaps, wire cutters to snip through barriers, and eventually tanks to crush the entanglements. For every innovation, defenders added more wire. Soldiers cursed it as "the Devil's wire," an enemy as deadly as the opposing army.

Wire transformed warfare from movement to siege, from quick victory to endless grinding. It represented the mechanization of killing, where industrial production methods created barriers that consumed human lives. A farmer's simple invention had become synonymous with mass death. The twisted metal reflected something twisted in human nature itself: our ability to turn any tool, no matter how innocent its origins, into an instrument of suffering.

The Global Spread

The 20th century saw barbed wire proliferate beyond battlefields into every form of human confinement. Nazi concentration camps were surrounded by electrified wire that killed anyone who touched it. Soviet gulags used wire to mark the boundaries of frozen labor camps. POW facilities, refugee camps, and political prisons all relied on Glidden's twisted strands to define the borders between freedom and captivity.

The Berlin Wall incorporated barbed wire into its death strip, where East German guards shot escapees tangled in the coils. Immigration facilities on every continent use wire to separate asylum seekers from their destinations. Modern prisons wrap their perimeters in concertina wire designed to slice anyone who attempts to climb it. Humanity had found its perfect technology: cheap, effective, and utterly indifferent to the suffering it caused.

Artists from Picasso to punk rockers adopted barbed wire as visual shorthand for oppression and confinement. It appears in protest art, album covers, and tattoos as a universal symbol of boundaries imposed by force. The wire speaks a language everyone understands: here freedom ends.

Today's borders bristle with sophisticated versions of Glidden's invention. The U.S.-Mexico frontier, the Hungarian-Serbian boundary, and Israel's security barriers all employ advanced wire systems with sensors, cameras, and automated alerts. What began as a tool to protect corn fields now monitors international borders, separating nations and peoples with industrial efficiency.

The environmental toll remains largely invisible but no less real. In winter, deer and moose become entangled in abandoned fence lines, unable to break free from the wire's grip. They starve slowly, their carcasses a reminder that the Devil's rope claims victims beyond the human species. Ranchers in Montana and Wyoming routinely find wildlife corpses twisted in old fencing, casualties of barriers that long outlive their original purpose.

This hidden slaughter speaks to something unsettling about barbed wire's persistence. Unlike wooden fences that rot or stone walls that crumble, wire endures for decades after abandonment. Drive through any rural area and you'll spot rusted strands still clinging to rotted posts, still capable of cutting flesh or trapping the unwary. The wire outlasts the farmers who strung it, the cattle it contained, and sometimes even the farms themselves. It might be the most successful product ever created, if success is measured by longevity and the ability to cause harm long after its usefulness has expired.

Joseph Glidden never imagined his agricultural innovation would become synonymous with human suffering. He designed wire to tame cattle and protect crops, creating prosperity through property rights and agricultural organization. The same invention that brought order to the American West became the infrastructure of oppression worldwide.

Twisted metal strands originally meant to give farmers control over their land evolved into humanity's preferred method of controlling people. From protecting wheat to imprisoning children, from stopping cattle to stopping refugees, barbed wire remains our most enduring symbol of separation. If there were awards for versatility in causing misery, barbed wire would sweep every category.

Every mile of wire tells two stories. One celebrates human ingenuity, the farmer's solution to an age-old problem of keeping animals where they belong. The other reveals humanity's capacity to transform any tool into an instrument of confinement. Glidden's "Winner" won by dividing the world into us and them, inside and outside, free and captive.

The Devil's rope continues marking where freedom ends and control begins, its barbs still sharp after 150 years of separating those who belong from those who don't. Glidden's creation tamed more than cattle; it tamed the human impulse to roam free.

Did You Know?

The Great Wall killed more people than barbed wire but took 2,000 years to build while barbed wire transformed warfare in 40 years. Glidden's invention was more efficient at spreading misery.

Modern razor wire has 3,000 cutting points per 100 feet, deadlier than WWI barbed wire. It's still just twisted metal - we've gotten better at making it hurt.

Pop Quiz: Who Am I? Historical Figures

History's greatest hits and worst villains, all playing the ultimate guessing game. Some conquered empires, others changed how we think, and a few just managed to get themselves killed in spectacular fashion.

Question 1

I was born in Corsica, crowned myself emperor, was mocked as being short (thanks, British propaganda), and was eventually defeated at Waterloo. **Who am I?**

Question 2

I was the last pharaoh of Egypt, spoke nine languages, had affairs with Julius Caesar and Mark Antony, and died from a snake bite (probably). **Who am I?**

Question 3

I was a lawyer who turned to armed resistance, spent 27 years breaking rocks in a quarry on a desolate island, and when freed at age 71, chose reconciliation over revenge. I shared a Nobel Prize with the man who once imprisoned me and danced at my 90th birthday party. **Who am I?**

Question 4

I discovered radium, was the first woman to win a Nobel Prize, won it twice in different fields, and my lab notebooks are still radioactive. **Who am I?**

Question 5

I was called "The Lady with the Lamp" for my nightly rounds in military hospitals. But my true weapon wasn't a lamp; it was a pie chart. By using statistics to prove that more soldiers died from disease than from battle wounds, I revolutionized modern medicine. **Who am I?**

Question 6

I crossed the Delaware, couldn't tell a lie about a cherry tree (which never happened), and became America's first president. **Who am I?**

Question 7

I sailed on the Beagle, wrote about evolution, and caused controversy by suggesting humans descended from apes. **Who am I?**

Question 8

"Workers of the world, unite! You have nothing to lose but your chains." I wrote Das Kapital, lived in poverty in London, and predicted the communist revolution. **Who am I?**

Question 9

I painted the Mona Lisa, designed flying machines, wrote backwards, and dissected corpses to understand anatomy. **Who am I?**

Question 10

I rode from the Gobi Desert to the Black Sea, forging the largest contiguous land empire in history. I was so successful in my conquests that the massive depopulation of my enemies allowed forests to regrow, removing so much carbon from the atmosphere that I actually cooled the planet. **Who am I?**

Question 11

I was crowned Holy Roman Emperor on Christmas Day 800 AD, united much of Western Europe, and couldn't read or write. **Who am I?**

Question 12

I conquered most of the known world by age 30, wept because there were no more worlds to conquer, and died mysteriously in Babylon. **Who am I?**

Question 13

I said "I am not a crook," resigned before impeachment, and opened diplomatic relations with China. **Who am I?**

Question 14

I was a doctor turned revolutionary, fought alongside Castro, was captured in Bolivia, and became a t-shirt icon after death. **Who am I?**

Question 15

"Veni, vidi, vici." I crossed the Rubicon, was stabbed 23 times in the Senate, and my name became the word for emperor. **Who am I?**

Question 16

I was educated in Paris, spoke fluent French, and dreamed of returning my country to a peasant paradise with no cities, no money, and no modern technology. My radical experiment to turn back the clock created "killing fields" and resulted in one of the 20th century's worst genocides. **Who am I?**

Question 17

I ruled the Soviet Union with an iron fist, starved millions in Ukraine, and was so paranoid I purged my own generals. **Who am I?**

Question 18

I was once a chicken farmer who became one of history's most evil men. I organized the Holocaust, was called "the architect of the Final Solution," carried a clipboard to genocide meetings like a bureaucrat, and killed myself with cyanide when captured. **Who am I?**

Question 19

"The unexamined life is not worth living." I never wrote anything down, was executed for corrupting youth, and my student Plato recorded my ideas about questioning everything. **Who am I?**

Question 20

I was a theoretical physicist who studied Sanskrit in my spare time and loved poetry. After witnessing a world-changing test in the New Mexico desert, I famously quoted the Bhagavad Gita, saying, "Now I am become Death, the destroyer of worlds." My conscience would later haunt me, and I spent years warning against the very weapons I helped create. **Who am I?**

Question 21

I was Henry VIII's second wife, had six fingers (maybe), was accused of adultery and witchcraft, and lost my head over it. **Who am I?**

Question 22

I sailed around the Pacific, mapped coastlines from New Zealand to Alaska, was killed in Hawaii, and have a group of islands named after me. **Who am I?**

Question 23

I was a mathematician who believed machines could think, created a test to prove it, and helped crack an "unbreakable" code during a world war. Despite saving countless lives with my work, my own government destroyed me for loving the wrong gender. I died eating a poisoned apple like Snow White. **Who am I?**

Question 24

I worked as a pastry chef in London and New York, adopted many aliases including "Uncle Chin," and founded a communist party while living in a cave. My guerrilla fighters wore sandals made from old tires and defeated two superpowers. **Who am I?**

Question 25

I composed nine symphonies, went deaf while writing music, and my "Ode to Joy" became the European Union's anthem. **Who am I?**

ANSWERS: Who Am I? Historical Figures

The masks are off, the mystery solved. Here are history's heavy hitters, complete with the messy truths textbooks usually skip.

1. Napoleon Bonaparte

Not the pint-sized villain of British cartoons; he stood about 5'7", average for his day. What set him apart was his appetite for conquest and his knack for rewriting Europe's map.

2. Cleopatra VII

The last ruler of Ptolemaic Egypt was Macedonian Greek, not ethnically Egyptian. She wasn't just a seductress; she was a master strategist who spoke nine languages and kept Egypt independent for decades.

3. Nelson Mandela

When he left Robben Island in 1990, he could have sought revenge. Instead, he built a democracy rooted in forgiveness, earning global respect and a Nobel Peace Prize.

4. Marie Curie

The only person to win Nobel Prizes in two different sciences, she discovered radium and polonium. Her old notebooks remain so radioactive you still need protective gear to read them.

5. Florence Nightingale

Her biggest weapon wasn't a lamp but a pie chart. She proved more soldiers were dying from disease than wounds, forcing the British government to revolutionize sanitation in hospitals.

6. George Washington

The first U.S. president never lived in the White House; it wasn't finished yet. His famous "wooden teeth" were actually made from ivory, gold, and even human teeth.

7. Charles Darwin

He delayed publishing *On the Origin of Species* for 20 years, fearing backlash. When he finally did, he sparked a debate that still rattles classrooms and pulpits today.

8. Karl Marx

He thundered about workers rising up but lived most of his life broke in London, relying on Engels to pay the bills. His writings outlived him by igniting revolutions worldwide.

9. Leonardo da Vinci

A polymath who painted the *Mona Lisa* and sketched flying machines centuries ahead of his time. He also dissected corpses in secret to understand the mechanics of life.

10. Genghis Khan

His empire stretched from China to Europe, the largest contiguous land empire ever. Genetic studies suggest millions of men today carry his DNA.

11. Charlemagne

Crowned on Christmas Day in 800, he united much of Western Europe. Ironically, while he pushed literacy and scholarship, he himself struggled with writing.

12. Alexander the Great

By 30 he had conquered Persia, Egypt, and beyond, founding more than 70 cities. He died mysteriously in Babylon; possibly poisoned, possibly from fever.

13. Richard Nixon

The only U.S. president to resign, he left office over Watergate. Yet he also opened relations with China, reshaping Cold War geopolitics.

14. Che Guevara

An Argentine doctor turned guerrilla, his image became a global symbol long after his death in Bolivia. Ironically, he disliked the celebrity status that made him an icon.

15. Julius Caesar

A general, dictator, and reformer, his assassination marked the end of the Roman Republic. His surname "Caesar" became a title for emperors for centuries after.

16. Pol Pot

Leader of the Khmer Rouge, his "Year Zero" campaign killed nearly two million Cambodians. Despite the devastation, he lived out his last years in quiet exile.

17. Joseph Stalin

A brutal dictator who oversaw purges, famines, and gulags, he also transformed the USSR into a superpower. He left behind a legacy of fear and industrial might.

18. Heinrich Himmler

Once a failed chicken farmer, he became head of the SS and architect of the Holocaust. His obsession with the occult sat uneasily beside his bureaucratic efficiency in genocide.

19. Socrates

The philosopher who wrote nothing, he left behind ideas through his student Plato. His death by hemlock made him a martyr for free inquiry.

20. J. Robert Oppenheimer

The "father of the atomic bomb" later spent his career warning against nuclear proliferation. He blended physics with philosophy, quoting Sanskrit texts as easily as equations.

21. Anne Boleyn

She helped spark England's break with the Catholic Church, but lost her life to accusations of treason. Her daughter Elizabeth went on to become one of England's greatest monarchs.

22. Captain James Cook

A master cartographer, he mapped more of the Pacific than anyone before him. His voyages reshaped Europe's understanding of the world but his final stop in Hawaii turned fatal.

23. Alan Turing

He cracked the Enigma code, shortening WWII and saving millions of lives. Postwar Britain repaid him with persecution for his sexuality, driving him to an early death.

24. Ho Chi Minh

Before leading Vietnam's fight for independence, he worked in kitchens in London and Paris. His guerrilla forces outlasted both French and American armies.

25. Ludwig van Beethoven

He went deaf yet composed some of the most powerful music ever written. His *Ode to Joy* now serves as Europe's anthem, a symbol of unity rising from turmoil.

Pop Quiz: Timeline Test, Chronology Challenge

Time waits for no one, but it sure loves to mess with your memory. Can you untangle these historical knots and put events in their proper order?

Question 1 Hitler's Rise to Power

1. Beer Hall Putsch in Munich
2. The Molotov–Ribbentrop Pact
3. Appointment as Chancellor of Germany
4. Publication of Mein Kampf
5. Night of the Long Knives

Question 2 The Soviet Union

1. The Great Purge
2. October Revolution in Petrograd
3. Treaty of Brest-Litovsk
4. Lenin's Death
5. Holodomor

Question 3 Revolutions of the World

1. The Iranian Revolution
2. The American Revolution

3. The Russian Revolution

4. The Haitian Revolution

5. The Chinese Communist Revolution

Question 4 Egyptian Rulers

1. Ramses the Great (Ramses II)

2. Cleopatra

3. Tutankhamun

4. Akhenaten

5. Thutmose III

Question 5 Financial Crises

1. Tulip Mania

2. European Sovereign Debt Crisis

3. The Great Depression

4. The South Sea Bubble

5. The Dot-Com Bubble

Question 6 U.S. Civil Rights Movement

1. Greensboro Sit-ins

2. March on Washington

3. Brown v. Board of Education

4. Montgomery Bus Boycott begins

5. MLK Jr. assassinated

Question 7 The Crusades

1. Constantinople is sacked during the Fourth Crusade

2. Saladin retakes Jerusalem

3. Pope Urban II calls for the First Crusade

4. Richard the Lionheart signs a truce with Saladin

5. Crusaders capture Jerusalem

Question 8 American Civil War

1. The Battle of Gettysburg

2. Abraham Lincoln is assassinated

3. Abraham Lincoln is elected President

4. Confederate forces fire on Fort Sumter

5. General Robert E. Lee surrenders at Appomattox Court House

Question 9 World War I

1. Germany signs the Treaty of Versailles

2. The United States enters the war

3. The Battle of the Somme

4. Assassination of Archduke Franz Ferdinand

5. Russia withdraws after the Bolshevik Revolution

Question 10 Artists by Birth Date

1. Pablo Picasso
2. Leonardo da Vinci
3. Vincent van Gogh
4. Edvard Munch
5. Andy Warhol

Question 11 War on Terror

1. Invasion of Iraq begins
2. Killing of Osama bin Laden
3. 9/11 terrorist attacks in the U.S.
4. U.S. and allies invade Afghanistan
5. Withdrawal of U.S. forces from Afghanistan

Question 12 The British Empire

1. Queen Victoria crowned Empress of India

2. American Revolution begins

3. Britain abolishes the slave trade

4. Sepoy Rebellion in India

5. Hong Kong handed back to China

Question 13 American Presidents by First Year in Office

1. Ulysses S. Grant elected
2. Theodore Roosevelt elected
3. Andrew Jackson elected
4. William McKinley elected
5. James Madison elected

Question 14 Cold War

1. SALT I (Strategic Arms Limitation Treaty) signed
2. Launch of Sputnik
3. Korean War begins
4. Cuban Missile Crisis
5. Marshall Plan announced in Europe

Question 15 Classic Films by Release

1. Casablanca

2. The Good, the Bad and the Ugly
3. 12 Angry Men
4. Seven Samurai
5. It's a Wonderful Life

Question 16 World War II

1. Neville Chamberlain resigns
2. D-Day landings in Normandy
3. Atomic bombings of Hiroshima and Nagasaki
4. Battle of Midway
5. German 6th Army surrenders at Stalingrad

Question 17 The French Revolution

1. Reign of Terror begins
2. Tennis Court Oath
3. Execution of Louis XVI
4. Storming of the Bastille
5. Napoleon's coup d'état

Question 18 Famous Plagues & Pandemics

1. HIV/AIDS identified
2. Plague of Justinian
3. COVID-19
4. Spanish Flu
5. Black Death in Europe

Question 19 Explorers of the World

1. Captain James Cook's first voyage departs
2. Ferdinand Magellan circumnavigation begins
3. Neil Armstrong walks on the Moon
4. Roald Amundsen reaches the South Pole
5. Christopher Columbus sails west

Question 20 Major Sports Moments

1. Babe Ruth's called shot
2. Serena Williams wins first Grand Slam
3. Jesse Owens wins 100m final in Berlin
4. Maradona's "Hand of God" goal
5. Miracle on Ice – U.S. beats USSR in hockey

Question 21 Women Who Made History

1. Amelia Earhart flies solo across the Atlantic

2. Rosa Parks sparks Montgomery Bus Boycott
3. Marie Curie wins Nobel Prize
4. Indira Gandhi becomes Prime Minister of India
5. Emmeline Pankhurst founds the Women's Social and Political Union (WSPU)

Question 22 The Napoleonic Era

1. Grande Armée crosses the Niemen into Russia
2. Napoleon abdicates and is exiled to Elba
3. Battle of Austerlitz
4. Napoleon crowned Emperor
5. Battle of Waterloo

Question 23 American Westward Expansion

1. Gold discovered at Sutter's Mill
2. Cherokee Removal (Trail of Tears) begins
3. Completion of the Transcontinental Railroad
4. Louisiana Purchase treaty signed
5. "Great Migration" sets out on the Oregon Trail

Question 24 Music History

1. Launch of MTV
2. The Beatles perform on The Ed Sullivan Show
3. Elvis releases "That's All Right"
4. Woodstock festival opens
5. Buddy Holly dies in a plane crash

Question 25 Natural Disasters

1. Tangshan earthquake
2. Hurricane Katrina
3. Yellow River flood
4. Chernobyl
5. Pompeii

ANSWERS: Timeline Test, Chronology Challenge

Chronology doesn't lie, unlike your confident guesses. Here's when things actually happened, with all the messy details time forgot to mention.

1. 1 (1923), 4 (1925), 3 (1933), 5 (1934), 2 (1939)

Hitler's beer hall flop landed him in jail, where he penned his infamous manifesto. His appointment as Chancellor was democracy's fatal mistake, followed by a bloody purge of rivals and a shocking handshake with Stalin.

2. 2 (1917), 3 (1918), 4 (1924), 5 (1932-33), 1 (1936-38)

The Bolsheviks stormed to power, quickly ditched WWI, then mourned Lenin's death. Stalin's man-made famine starved millions before his paranoid purges eliminated anyone who might threaten his grip on power.

3. 2 (1775), 4 (1791), 3 (1917), 5 (1949), 1 (1979)

Americans rebelled against tea taxes, Haiti's slaves broke their chains, Russians toppled their Tsar, Mao's peasants conquered China, and Iranians traded a Shah for an Ayatollah.

4. 5 (1479-1425 BCE), 4 (1353-1336 BCE), 3 (1332-1323 BCE), 1 (1279-1213 BCE), 2 (69-30 BCE)

NOTE - For ancient history dates like those for Egyptian rulers, we use BCE (Before Common Era), which is the same as BC. The years countdown to year 1. This means a larger number, like 1353 BCE, is older than a smaller number, like 69 BCE.

Egypt's greatest warrior-pharaoh expanded the empire, then came the heretic king who worshipped one god. The boy-king's tomb survived tomb robbers, Ramses built monuments everywhere, and Cleopatra seduced Rome but lost everything.

5. 1 (1630s), 4 (1720), 3 (1929), 5 (1990s-2000), 2 (2009)

Dutch tulip bulbs became worth more than houses until reality hit. British investors got burned by South Sea stocks, then the world crashed in '29. Dot-com dreams turned to nightmares, and Europe's debt chickens came home to roost.

6. 3 (1954), 4 (1955-56), 1 (1960), 2 (1963), 5 (1968)

The Supreme Court outlawed school segregation, Rosa Parks sparked a boycott revolution, students sat down to stand up, MLK had a dream on the Washington steps, then an assassin's bullet silenced the movement's greatest voice.

7. 3 (1095), 5 (1099), 2 (1187), 4 (1192), 1 (1204)

The Pope called for holy war, Crusaders bathed Jerusalem in blood, Saladin took it back with style, Richard settled for a truce, then the Fourth Crusade forgot about Muslims and sacked a Christian city instead.

8. 3 (1860), 4 (1861), 1 (1863), 5 (1865), 2 (1865)

Lincoln's election split the nation, Fort Sumter's cannons started the bloodbath, Gettysburg turned the tide after three days of carnage, Lee surrendered with dignity, then Booth's bullet made Lincoln a martyr.

9. 4 (1914), 3 (1916), 2 (1917), 5 (1918), 1 (1919)

An archduke's assassination lit Europe's powder keg, the Somme became a meat grinder for nothing, America finally joined the party, Russia quit after their revolution, and Versailles planted seeds for the next war.

10. 2 (1452), 3 (1853), 4 (1863), 1 (1881), 5 (1928)

Renaissance genius Leonardo mastered everything, Van Gogh painted madness beautifully, Munch captured existential dread in a scream, Picasso shattered art into cubes, and Warhol turned soup cans into high art.

11. 3 (2001), 4 (2001), 1 (2003), 2 (2011), 5 (2021)

Planes became weapons in Manhattan's towers, America invaded Afghanistan hunting bin Laden, then got distracted by Iraq's phantom WMDs, finally killed their most wanted man, and fled Kabul in chaos twenty years later.

12. 2 (1775), 3 (1807), 4 (1857), 1 (1876), 5 (1997)

Colonists revolted against the Crown, Britain abolished its slave trade, Indian sepoys mutinied against their masters, Victoria became Empress of the jewel in the crown, and Hong Kong returned to China after 156 years.

13. 5 (1808), 3 (1828), 1 (1868), 4 (1896), 2 (1901)

Madison led the young republic, Jackson brought frontier democracy to Washington, Grant the war hero became a peacetime disappointment, McKinley rode prosperity until an anarchist's bullet. Theodore Roosevelt took office in 1901 after the assassination of President McKinley.

14. 5 (1947), 2 (1957), 3 (1950), 4 (1962), 1 (1972)

America offered Europe a Marshall Plan lifeline, Russia shocked the world with Sputnik, Korea became the first hot war of the Cold War, nuclear missiles in Cuba nearly ended everything, and Nixon signed arms control with the Soviets.

15. 5 (1946), 1 (1942), 4 (1954), 3 (1957), 2 (1966)

Capra showed us what wonderful lives we have, Casablanca proved love conquers all in wartime, Kurosawa's samurai epic influenced every Western, 12 angry men deliberated justice to perfection, and Eastwood made spaghetti Westerns cool.

16. 1 (1940), 4 (1942), 5 (1943), 2 (1944), 3 (1945)

Chamberlain's appeasement failed and he resigned, Japan's naval dominance died at Midway, Hitler's 6th Army froze to death at Stalingrad, D-Day opened Europe's second front, and atomic fire ended the Pacific war.

17. 2 (1789), 4 (1789), 3 (1793), 1 (1793), 5 (1799)

Tennis Court Oath started the revolution, the Bastille's fall made it real, the king lost his head to the guillotine, Robespierre's Reign of Terror consumed its own children, then Napoleon's coup ended the chaos with dictatorship.

18. 2 (541-549), 5 (1347-1351), 4 (1918-1919), 1 (1981), 3 (2019)

Justinian's plague weakened the Byzantine Empire, the Black Death killed a third of Europe, Spanish flu slaughtered more than the Great War, AIDS emerged from the shadows, and COVID shut down the modern world.

19. 5 (1492), 2 (1519), 1 (1768), 4 (1911), 3 (1969)

Columbus sailed west and found a new world by accident, Magellan started the first round-the-world trip (though he didn't finish it), Cook mapped the Pacific's islands, Amundsen planted Norway's flag at the South Pole, and Armstrong took mankind's giant leap.

20. 3 (1936), 1 (1932), 5 (1980), 4 (1986), 2 (1999)

Jesse Owens embarrassed Hitler's master race theory in Berlin, Babe Ruth allegedly called his shot in Yankee Stadium, amateur Americans stunned the Soviet hockey machine, Maradona's hand fooled the referee against England, and teenage Serena won her first Grand Slam.

21. 5 (1903), 3 (1903), 1 (1932), 2 (1955), 4 (1966)

Emmeline founded the suffragette movement in Britain, Marie Curie became the first woman to win a Nobel Prize, Amelia Earhart flew solo across the Atlantic, Rosa Parks sparked a bus boycott revolution, and Indira Gandhi became India's Iron Lady.

22. 4 (1804), 3 (1805), 1 (1812), 2 (1814), 5 (1815)

Napoleon crowned himself Emperor in Notre Dame, Austerlitz proved his military genius against Austria and Russia, winter and distance crushed his Russian invasion, he abdicated to Elba after Paris fell, then Waterloo ended his Hundred Days comeback.

23. 4 (1803), 5 (1843), 2 (1838), 1 (1848), 3 (1869)

Jefferson doubled America's size with the Louisiana Purchase, pioneers followed the Oregon Trail seeking new lives, Cherokee were forced from their homeland on the Trail of Tears, California gold sparked the '49er rush, and the transcontinental railroad united the coasts.

24. 3 (1954), 2 (1964), 4 (1969), 5 (1959), 1 (1981)

Elvis released his first single and changed everything, the Beatles invaded America on Ed Sullivan, Woodstock defined the counterculture generation, a plane crash made Buddy Holly's music immortal, and MTV brought music to television.

25. 5 (79 CE), 3 (1931), 2 (1976), 4 (1986), 1 (2005)

Vesuvius buried Pompeii in ash for eternity, China's Yellow River drowned millions in floods, Tangshan's earthquake flattened a city overnight, Chernobyl's reactor melted down and poisoned the future, and Katrina drowned New Orleans while America watched.

Scan the QR code and join our FREE weekly newsletter.

Every week you'll get fresh quizzes, mind-bending facts, and hilarious history stories delivered straight to your inbox. It's like keeping the fun of this book going, long after you've closed the cover

We'll even send you an exclusive peek at our Amazon #1 Bestseller, Shut the Fact Up.

No spam, no boring stuff. Just facts that surprise, delight, and occasionally make you laugh out loud.

Scan the QR code and start your weekly trivia fix today!

Last Call at the History Tavern

First things first…

Thank you for making it all the way here. You could have been scrolling your phone, bingeing another show, or arguing on the internet about who really built the pyramids, but instead, you chose to hang out with us in the past. That means more than you know.

We're a small, independent crew with one big goal: to serve up history in a way that's fun, surprising, and easy to digest. No dusty textbooks, no yawns, just the good stuff, trimmed of excess, spiced with wit, and poured straight into your brain like a fine ale.

If you had a good time, the best way to keep this going is simple: leave a quick review. It helps new readers discover us, and it gives us the fuel to keep digging up stories, strange facts, and quiz-worthy gems.

Printed in Dunstable, United Kingdom